T0248134

EVERY PERSON'S GUIDE TO JEWISH BLESSINGS

Every Person's Guide to Jewish Blessings

Ron Isaacs

KTAV PUBLISHING HOUSE

Every Person's Guide to Jewish Blessings

KTAV PUBLISHING HOUSE

527 Empire Blvd

Brooklyn, NY 11225

www.ktav.com

orders@ktav.com

Ph: (718) 972-5449 / Fax: (718) 972-6307

Typeset by Raphaël Freeman MISTD, Renana Typesetting

ISBN 978-1-60280-428-9

Printed and bound in the United States of America

Contents

For Evie, our newest blessing

Acknowledgements

I wish to express my thanks to Moshe Heller, CEO of Ktav who has continued the legacy of a publisher which has provided countless high-quality books for its readers. I also want to express my gratitude to Shira Atwood who has been gracious in answering my questions in a timely manner and whose artistic creativity helped to shape the book's cover. The typesetter, Raphael Freeman, MISTD (Renana Typesetting), has done a magnificent job in creating a very readable volume. And last by certainly not least, I want to thank my beloved wife Leora for her many hours of work in editing my manuscript and offering many constructive suggestions. She is truly my woman of valor.

Introduction

The building block of all Jewish prayer is the blessing. The blessings pronounced on various occasions are attributed to the Men of the Great Assembly (400–300 BCE), the spiritual leaders in the time of Ezra the Scribe. Blessings were formulated for practically every contingency: for the usual experiences of daily life, such as arising from sleep, dressing, eating, and drinking, and for the unusual happenings, such as escaping from danger, recovering from illness, or seeing something wondrous in nature.

The Hebrew word for blessing, *beracha*, is generally understood to be derived from the Hebrew word *berech* meaning 'knee.' The bending of the knee while praying was one of the ways of honoring God. The Rasba, a Talmudic scholar, has said that the word *berach* is derived from the Hebrew word *bereicha* which means a spring of water. Just as a spring flows constantly and its waters increase, so too, when we bless God we are proclaiming our desire to display God's ever-increasing presence in the world.

Living life is a magnificent gift. The Judaic teachers have taught people to mark their time by saying blessings. What is a blessing? A blessing is generally understood to be anything that begins with these six Hebrew words:

Baruch Ata Adonai Eloheinu melech ha'olam

Praised are You, Lord our God, Ruler of the Universe...

Every moment of our lives counts. The Jewish practice of saying daily blessings derives from the desire to promote joy and appreciation, wonder and thankfulness, amazement, and praise. By noticing our gifts in life each day, we are striving for a place of holiness.

From Bible times to the present, Jews have used blessings to consecrate special moments in our lives. Rabbi Meir, one of the great Talmudic sages of bygone years, used to say: 'A person should say one hundred blessings each day' (*Talmud, Menachot 43b*). According to Rabbi Meir, saying one hundred blessings a day will help one master the virtue of awe and reverence. If each of us were to take notice of one hundred things in our lives each day we would be much more mindful of everything around us.

Every Person's Guide to Jewish Blessings is a comprehensive anthology of information related to the blessings, their sources, and their uses in Jewish life. It includes laws and customs related to the entire gamut of blessings, a section on the life cycle blessings of circumcision, *pidyon haben, Bar/Bat Mitzvah,* seven wedding blessings of marriage, blessings for conversion, a chapter on the priestly blessing and how it evolved into the family blessing on Sabbath eve, and information related to the *Torah* blessings, the blessing after the meal, food blessings, blessings of enjoyment, (taste and smell) blessing of the sun and moon, a variety of liturgical blessings and blessing curiosities (*e.g.*, the only five blessings that are recited only once a year). There are also sections on rabbinic legends related to blessings, notable blessing quotations and a blessing glossary.

I fervently hope that this book will inspire you to use the gift of blessings throughout your life by noticing what is happening around you and showing appreciation by reciting blessings. Look for these opportunities and take time to express your gratitude with a blessing. May you count your one hundred blessings every day!

Ronald H. Isaacs

Blessings: A Brief History

The building block of all Jewish prayer is the blessing. The liturgical formula referring to the praise of God is the main source of all the poetry that was composed and added to the prayer book over the centuries. The blessings pronounced on various occasions are attributed in the Talmud (*Berachot 33a*) to the Men of the Great Assembly (400 to 300 BCE), the spiritual leaders in the time of Ezra the Scribe, who are considered to be the successors of the prophets in that they kept alive the knowledge of the Torah and Jewish traditions. Others ascribe the institution and formulae of the blessings to the sages of old (*Sifre Deuteronomy 33:2*) or to the 120 elders at the head of the community in the time of Ezra (*Talmud Megillah 17b*).

The Bible makes mention of a number of individual blessings. In almost all cases they are said to God in thanksgiving for some wondrous or good deed that God has performed for a person or persons. Here is a brief summary of them:

1. *Genesis 24:27:* And he [Eliezer] said: 'Blessed be the Lord, the God of my master Abraham, who has not forsaken His mercy and His truth toward my master...'
2. *Exodus 18:10:* And Jethro [father-in-law] of Moses said: Blessed be the Lord, who has delivered you out of the hand of the Egyptians, and out of the hand of Pharaoh; who has delivered the people from under the hand of the Egyptians.
3. *Ruth 4:14:* And the women said to Naomi: 'Blessed be the Lord, who has not withheld a redeemer from you today. May his name be perpetuated in Israel.'

4. *I Samuel 25:32, 33:* David said to Abigail: 'Blessed be the Lord, the God of Israel, who sent you this day to meet me. And blessed be your prudence, and blessed be you yourself for restraining me from seeking redress in blood by my own hands.

5. *II Samuel 18:28:* Ahimaaz called out and said to the king: 'All is well.' He bowed low with his face to the ground and said, 'Blessed be the Lord your God, who has delivered up the men who raised their hand against my lord the king.'

6. *I Kings 1:48:* This is what the king said, 'Blessed be the Lord, the God of Israel who has this day provided a successor to my throne, while my own eyes can see it.'

7. *I Kings 5:21:* When Hiram heard Solomon's message, he was overjoyed. 'Blessed be the Lord this day,' he said, 'for granting David a wise son to govern this great people.'

8. *I Kings 8:15:* The king [Solomon] said: 'Praised be the Lord, the God of Israel, who has fulfilled with deeds the promise He made to my father David.'

9. *I Kings 8:56:* He [Solomon] stood and in a loud voice blessed the whole congregation of Israel: 'Blessed be the Lord who has granted a haven to His people Israel, just as He promised, not a single word has failed of all the gracious promises that God made through His servant Moses.'

10. *I Chronicles 16:36:* Blessed is the Lord, God of Israel, from eternity to eternity.

11. *II Chronicles 2:11:* Hiram continued, 'Praised is the Lord, God of Israel, who made the heavens and earth, who gave King David a wise son, endowed with intelligence and understanding, to build a House for the Lord and a royal palace for himself.

12. *II Chronicles 6:4:* He [Solomon] said: 'Praised is the Lord God of Israel, who made a promise to my father David and fulfilled it.'

13. *Psalms 28:6:* Blessed is the Lord, for God listens to my plea of mercy.

14. *Psalms 31:22:* Blessed be the Lord, for God has been wondrously faithful to me, a veritable bastion.

The Apocryphal Books of the Bible also contain individual blessings. After the victory of the Maccabees over Nicanor, the people exclaimed, 'Blessed be the One who has kept His holy place undefiled.' (*II Maccabees 15:34*). And according to the book of *Enoch* (*36:4*), each time Enoch beheld some of the wonders of nature he blessed the Lord of Glory, who had made great and glorious wonders to show the greatness of His work to the angels and to spirits and to men, that they might praise His work and all His creation.

Maimonides, the great medieval codifier, writes in his *Mishneh Torah*: 'The formulae of all blessings have come down from Ezra and his counsel. It is improper to change them, to add to or subtract from anything in the phrasing of one of them. Whoever deviates from the form which the sages have given to the blessings falls into error.'

Blessings were formulated for practically every contingency: for the usual experiences of daily life, such as arising from sleep, dressing, eating, and drinking, and for the unusual happenings, such as escaping from danger, recovering from illness, hearing of the death of a loved one, or seeing something wondrous in nature.

Sefer HaChinuch, the classic thirteenth-century work on the six hundred and thirteen commandments, analyzes the meaning of the word *baruch*. (*No. 430*). Since all honor and all wisdom and all blessing reside solely in God, nothing that man says or does can add to God any such qualities. It is presumptuous to think that God's blessing is increased on account of our prayers. *Baruch* should therefore be regarded as descriptive of God. Just as God is an *El rachum vechanun* (a merciful and compassionate God), God is also an *El Baruch* (a blessed God). As mercy and compassion flow from God, so does all blessing. *Baruch Ata Adonai* basically then means that 'You O God are the source, the fountainhead of all blessing.'

As to the number of blessings required for daily recitation, Rabbi Meir, a second-century scholar, stated that it is the duty of every Jew to recite one hundred blessings daily.

ORIGIN OF THE *BERACHOT*

Many scholars have shown that the various blessings were likely to have originated in different congregations and localities. The formulas that were eventually adopted by the Jewish people as a whole were selections from and combinations of local customs and traditions. Any attempts of other scholars to establish a definitive date for the formulation of each blessing and to reconstruct an original wording appear to lack foundation.

There are numerous indications which suggest that different formulas were known and used simultaneously. For example, similarities to the eighteen blessings which comprise the *Amidah* prayer are to be found in various sources, including the hymn recorded in *Ecclesiasticus 51:12* and the prayer found in *Ecclesiasticus* 36. Like the *Amidah*, *Ecclesiasticus* 36 also contains a series of blessings petitioning for the ingathering of the exiles and the salvation of Israel.

END OF THE SECOND TEMPLE PERIOD

By the end of the period of the Second Temple, certain orders of blessings had become the generally accepted custom in most communities. These included the seven blessings which comprise the Sabbath and Festival *Amidah* prayer, and the nine blessings for Rosh Hashanah (*Tosef., Berachot 3:14*), and most likely also the eighteen blessings for the weekday Amidah. The number and contents of the blessings before and after the Shema prayer and the three blessings of the Blessings after the Meal were also standardized at about this time. The redaction of the regular prescribed prayers and blessings under Rabban Gamaliel II at Yavneh (*Talmud Berachot* 28b) at the end of the first century of the common era gave official sanction to what had been in essence the prevailing custom for a considerable time, and probably established the order and content of the blessings. It did not, however, become the single authoritative version.

THE TALMUDIC PERIOD

At the earliest, prayers were written down by the end of the Talmudic period, and many alternate formulations of the same blessing are known from Talmudic sources. Some are in use in different rites to the present day. The order of prayer was still relatively flexible, and blessings were well defined, although their recital still involved some improvisation in order that they not become overly rote and mechanical. Some Amoraim were singled out for praise because they recited a new blessing every day. (*Jerusalem Talmud, Berachot 4:3*)

However, during the time of the Talmud, only the requirements for the wording of each blessing were fixed in great detail. Consistent attempts at establishing one single authoritative version of all prayers only came later.

The Blessing Formula

Every blessing opens with the Hebrew words *Baruch Ata Adonai* (Praised are You, O God). When the blessing occurs at the beginning of a prayer, the words *Eloheinu melech ha'olam* (our God, Sovereign of the Universe) are added. The longest form of the blessing are those recited in conjunction with the performance of a specific mitzvah (religious obligation). It adds the Hebrew phrase *asher kidshanu b'mitzvotav v'tzivanu* (who has sanctified us with His commandments and commanded us to . . .). One interesting feature of this longer blessing formula is the switch within the blessing from second-person voice to third person. At the beginning, God is addressed directly: 'Praised are You.' This is immediately followed by a change of the person of the blessing from second to third, when speaking about God: 'who sanctified us with His commandments.' This change allows for the realization on the part of the person uttering the blessing that God is both near and far – or, in theological terms, both 'immanent' and 'transcendent.' Abudarham, a fourteenth century scholar, relates the use of both the second and third person in the blessing to the hidden and revealed aspects of God. To that which God reveals, we use the more familiar second person, while the third person reminds us that God's essence will always remain a mystery.

Also commenting on the formula of the blessing, Rabbi David ben Joseph once said: 'We begin the blessing with the words 'Praised be You, O Lord our God,' in order to remind ourselves that the God we worship is our God and the God of all people. Then we say, 'Ruler of the Universe,' to remember that our God is also the Power which sustains all of nature.'

THE SIX BLESSING WORDS

It is usually suggested that the word *baruch* comes from a root used in the Hebrew word *berech* (knee) and that *baruch* has something to do with bowing or bending the knee. This is a very uncertain theory. *Baruch* may simply come from a word in another ancient language which also means to praise or to bless. Today, most liturgists assert that the word *baruch* implies that God is deserving of man's praise.

The Hebrew word *ata* means you, and thus in reciting a blessing one enters into a relationship with God. The famous modern Jewish philosopher Martin Buber spoke of two main kinds of relationships which he called the 'I-It' and 'I-Thou'. An example of an I-It Relationship is the relationship between a thing and a person. Thus, a person who sits on a chair has entered into an I-It relationship with the chair, an object with which one cannot enter into dialogue.

The other type of relationship, an I-Thou involves human beings related to one another with the sum of their relationship being much greater than the sum of the parts. The relationship of a person to God is an I-Thou relationship. Such a relationship is much more intense and likely to evolve and grow as time goes on.

The Hebrew word *Adonai* is often translated as Lord. Adonai as it is used in the blessing formula is really the personal name of the God of Israel. It literally means 'my master' or 'my lord', and Jewish rabbinic tradition has come to associate this word for God to represent God's qualities of mercy.

The Hebrew word *Eloheinu*, the fourth word in the blessing formula means 'our God.' It is based on the Hebrew word *Elohim*, a more general term for God. Jewish tradition has come to associate the word *Eloheinu* to represent God's attributes of justice.

The Hebrew word *melech* means 'king' or sovereign. It implies that God rules over all, and just as a king has subjects who are subservient to him, so too does God have the people who are His servants.

Finally, the Hebrew word *ha'olam* means the world or the universe. Thus God is the God of everything that is.

THREE TYPES OF BLESSING FORMULAS

There are three types of formulas for blessings. The first is a short blessing, called in Hebrew *matbe'ah katzar* – 'short formula', which, after its opening of *Baruch Ata Adonai* is followed by a few words of praise specific to the occasion. For example, in the blessing over wine, we say the following: *Baruch Ata Adonai Eloheinu melech ha'olam boray pri hagafen* – Praised are You, God, Lord of the Universe, who creates the fruit of the vine.

The second blessing formula is a long blessing (*matbe'a aroch*), in which the opening of the blessing is followed by a more elaborate text. An example is the first section of the Blessing after the Meal, after which a concluding blessing formula must be recited at the end of the prayer (*e.g., Baruch Ata Adonai, hazan et ha-kol* – Praised are You, Lord, who feeds all).

The third type of blessing forms part of a series (called in Hebrew *beracha ha-semucha le-chaverta* – 'contiguous blessing') Here, the opening formula is omitted (except in the first blessing of each series) and only the conclusion is phrased in the blessing style. An example of this type of formula is the second section of the Blessing after the Meal, which begins with the Hebrew words *nodeh lecha* (We thank You) and ends with the blessing *Baruch Ata Adonai al ha'aretz ve-al ha-mazon* – Praised are You, O God, for the land and the food. (*Jerusalem Talmud* 1:8, 3d)

The reference to God as *Melech Ha'olam* (Sovereign of the Universe) occurs only in the first two blessing formulas, and not in the third. It is totally absent from the *Amidah* prayer, and it is conjectured that it probably did not become customary before the second century of the Common Era. Some say that the introduction of the phrase 'Sovereign of the Universe' may have been prompted by the desire to stress the exclusive sovereignty of God as a polemic against the Roman cult of worship of the emperor.

In all of the Bible, the standard blessing formula occurs only twice:

1. *Psalms 119:12*: Blessed are You, O God, train me in Your laws.
2. *1 Chronicles 29:10*: David said, 'Blessed are You, Lord, God of Israel our father, from eternity to eternity.'

The Talmud retains some traces of formulas other than the standard ones. For example, in the tractate *Berachot 40b*, Benjamin the shepherd made a sandwich and said, 'Blessed be the Master of this bread' and Rav said that Benjamin had performed his obligation. It was also taught that if a person sees a fig and says: 'What a fine fig this is. Blessed be the Omnipresent that has created it,' he has performed his obligation.

PURPOSES OF BLESSINGS

The genius of the blessing formula is the opportunity it provides for the worshipper to establish a close relationship with God by speaking to Him directly. Dr. Steve Brown, in his book *Higher and Higher: Making Prayer a Part of Us* (United Synagogue Department of Youth), identifies several important purposes of the blessing formula:

- To thank God for the blessings that a person has received.
- To assume an ethical responsibility for our blessings. For example, when one recites a blessing thanking God for giving bread, there ought to be an expectation of taking on an ethical responsibility for one's food, which would include not wasting food. In addition, saying a blessing over food might be an excellent reminder of one's own bounty, and perhaps might stimulate one to be reminded of one's ethical responsibility to feed the hungry.
- To help sensitize people to the beauty and joy of the world that God has given people. By saying 'thank you' to God for one's blessings, a person does not take life and life's blessings for granted.
- To help imbue an experience with spirituality. Reciting blessings helps a person to change the common variety of experience, raising it, and, in the process, making a person closer to the image of God. A good example of the spiritualizing experience of a blessing relates to blessings over food. Here people that say blessings have an opportunity to elevate their eating experience by thanking God for the pleasures involved in tasting and eating food. In addition, reciting a blessing over food slows down the process of eating and

allows a person to think about the food that he or she is about to eat and appreciate it that much more. The Talmud says that the table upon which one eats is like the altar of the Temple. By reciting blessings the whole process of eating is changed into a beautiful ceremony. Washing hands before eating and saying a blessing is a reminder of the ancient priests who washed their hands before they offered a sacrifice. Every home has the potential to make its table an altar, every meal a sacrifice and every Jew a priest. By saying blessings Judaism takes the routine act of eating and raises it to lofty heights, to the domain of the holy and sacred. Abraham Joshua Heschel gave classic expression to this thought when he wrote that 'perhaps the essential message of Judaism is that in doing the finite, we can perceive the infinite.' Even in eating a slice of bread, one can discover God!

The Laws of the Blessings

Many of the rabbinic discussions of blessings are contained in the *Mishnah* tractate *Berachot* and the *Gemara* in both the *Jerusalem* and *Babylonian Talmud*. Following is a synopsis of some of the laws of blessings and their recitation.

The *Talmud* (*Berachot 40b*) quotes the teacher Rav as saying that every blessing must have the name of God, and Rabbi Yochanan as saying that each blessing must also contain the attribute of God's kingship. It is also understood from this Talmudic passage that one could recite a blessing in the vernacular and it did not have to be an exact translation of the Hebrew formula. In the *Talmud* (*Berachot 40b*), a shepherd is quoted as saying in Aramaic, 'Blessed be God, the master of this bread,' and Rav agreed that it was sufficient.

While the blessing formula is obligatory in every one of the prescribed prayers, its use is precluded in spontaneous free prayers: 'One who recites a blessing which is not necessary is considered to transgress the prohibition 'You shall not take the name of the Lord Your God in vain'' (*Exodus 20:7*; *Talmud Berachot 33a*).

In his *Mishneh Torah* Maimonides divides the benedictions into three types: those which are recited before enjoying something pleasurable (*e.g.,* food); those which are recited for the performance of a religious duty (*e.g.,* hearing the shofar); and those which are forms of liturgical thanksgiving and praise (*e.g.,* Blessing after the Meal).

Abudarham distinguished four classes of blessings: those recited in the daily prayers, those preceding the performance of a religious duty, blessings offered for enjoyment and those of thanksgiving or praise.

Many blessings, though obligatory and therefore couched in the characteristic blessing formula, are not recited in congregational worship but by the individual in private prayer. Prominent among them are three groups: blessings before and after partaking of food and drink; blessings to be recited before the performance of most *mitzvot,* and blessings of praise for various occasions (the blessings of the morning which express one's gratitude for awakening each morning in possession of all of one's faculties were originally of this type). Since all three types of blessings are essentially of a private character, no minyan (quorum of ten adults) is required for their recitation. (The Blessing after the Meal is, however, preceded by a special introduction when said in the company of a quorum (*i.e.,* ten adults).

All blessings recited before the observance of a *mitzvah* (religious obligation) begins with the formula 'Blessed are You, Lord our God, Ruler of the Universe, who has sanctified us through His commandments and commanded us...' and mention the specific mitzvah about to be performed. The same formula is also used before the performance of commandments of rabbinic origin, such as the lighting of candles on the Sabbath or Festivals or on Hanukkah. These commandments are implied in the biblical injunction to observe the teaching of the sages (*Deuteronomy 17:10*).

The actual blessing over the *mitzvah* is sometimes followed by further blessings. For instance, on lighting the Hanukkah candles the blessing 'who has performed miracles for our fathers in days of old at this season' is recited. When a *mitzvah* is performed for the first time in the year, the *shehecheyanu* blessing ('who has kept us alive, and sustained us, and enabled us to reach this season) is also added.

No blessings are recited after the observance of *mitzvot,* unless they involve public reading from the Bible (e.g. Torah, Prophets, Hallel Psalms of Praise).

In practice, a blessing is not recited before the performance of every *mitzvah.* Some commentators have suggested that the determining principle is that no blessing should be recited before *mitzvot* which do not involve any action (*e.g.,* leaving the corner of the field for the poor (*Leviticus 19:9*) or the observance of which is possible only in undesirable circumstances (*e.g.,* divorce).

According to Rabbi Meir, it is the duty of every Jewish person to recite one hundred blessings each day (*Talmud Menachot 43b*), a custom which, according to one tradition, was instituted by King David (*Midrash, Numbers Rabbah 18:21*).

Following are some other laws of blessings as culled from the *Code of Jewish Law* (Condensed Version):

1. Before uttering any blessing, we must make sure which one it is, so that when we mention God's name, which is the most important part of the blessing, we shall know what we are thanking God for. It is forbidden to do anything else while reciting a blessing. And it must not be uttered hurriedly. But attention must be paid to the meaning of the words. And this is what the *Book of the Pious* says: 'When we wash our hands, or utter a benediction over fruit, or over a precept – benedictions which everybody knows, we must direct our attention to praise the name of our Creator, who was wondrously kind to us in giving us the fruit or the bread of which we partake, and in commanding us to perform this precept. We must not do it automatically out of sheer habit, spouting words thoughtlessly. On account of this, the anger of God was kindled, and God sent us word by Isaiah His prophet saying (*Isaiah 29:13*): 'For as much as this people draw near, with their mouths and their lips do honor Me, and their fear of Me is but the acquired precept of men.' The Holy Blessed One, said to Isaiah: 'Look at the deeds of My children, and see that they do it only outwardly, and hold on to it just as a man clings to the practices of his forefathers. They enter My house and pray to Me the fixed prayers, in accordance with the customs of their fathers, but not with their whole hearts. They wash their hands and utter the blessing for the occasion. They cut off a piece of bread and recite the blessing *hamotzi*. They drink and pronounce blessings habitually, but at the time they do not intend to praise Me by it.' Therefore, God's wrath was kindled and God swore by His great name to destroy the wisdom of their wise men, who know God and praise God because of established customs, but not wholeheartedly, as it is written: 'Therefore, behold, I will do yet farther... so that the wisdom of their wise men shall be lost,'

etc. Therefore have the Sages warned us concerning this matter, saying (*Nedarim* 62a): 'Do things for the sake of their Maker.' A man should accustom himself to say the blessings aloud, because an audible voice is conducive to concentration of mind.

2. When we say a blessing, our mouths must be free of saliva, nor should anything else be in our mouths, for it is said: *Psalms 71:8*: 'My mouth shall be filled with Your praise.'

3. It is forbidden to utter the name of God in vain, and whoever utters it in vain is guilty of violating a Divine Command, for it is written (*Deuteronomy 6:13*): 'You shall fear the Lord your God;' and it is written again (*Deuteronomy 28:58*): 'If you will not observe...to fear this glorious and fearful Name.' Included in the concept of fear is, that one should not mention God's great Name unless it is by the way of praise or blessing whenever required, or when studying the Torah. One's entire body must tremble upon mentioning the name of God, blessed be His name, but one should not mention it in vain, God forbid. This injunction applies not only to the ineffable Name (the four letters *Yod, Hey, Vav, Hey* – the Tetragrammaton), but to all attributes of God, Blessed be the One. It is forbidden to mention the Name not only in the Holy Tongue (Hebrew), but in any language. He who in any language curses himself or his neighbor by pronouncing the ineffable Name or one of God's attributes (an 'attribute' is a word or phrase by which we praise the Holy One, blessed be He, such as, 'the Great,' 'the Mighty,' 'the Revered,' 'the Faithful,' 'the Glorious,' 'the Strong,' 'the Steadfast,' 'the Omnipresent,' 'the Gracious,' 'the Merciful,' 'the Zealous,' 'the Long suffering,' 'the Abundant in mercy,') is liable to the penalty of lashes. Due to our sinful propensities, most people are careless and say in the vernacular, 'God shall punish him,' or the like, thus violating a Divine Command. If one curses without mentioning the ineffable Name of God, or one of His attributes, or if the curse can be inferred from the contents of one's words, as for instance when one says: 'May that man not be blessed by God,' or using expressions of similar nature, although one does not incur the punishment of lashes in this instance, nevertheless it constitutes

a violation. It is likewise forbidden to incorporate His name, may God be blessed, in a letter, no matter in what language it is written. Many people erroneously write His name, may He be blessed, in the vernacular, or they write the word adieu, which in the French language means 'with God;' this constitutes a clear violation, for in the course of time, this letter will be thrown on a dunghill. The mentioning of God's name frequently, especially when mentioned disdainfully, God forbid, causes poverty in Israel. And wisdom and endeavor are required to abolish this evil. When saliva accumulates in one's mouth, one should spit it out first and then mention the name of God. Likewise, when one is about to kiss the Scroll of the Law, one should first spit out his saliva. When we wish to mention the name of God in our daily talk, we are to say *Hashem* (the Name) and not as the common people say *Adoshem*, for this is undignified when referring to Heaven.

4. Great care should be taken not to utter a benediction in vain, God forbid; nor should one create for oneself an occasion over which to utter an unnecessary blessing. If by inadvertence we do utter a blessing in vain, or we mention the name of God unnecessarily, we should thereafter say: *Baruch shem kevod malchuto le'olam va'ed* (Blessed be the name of His glorious kingdom forever and ever). If immediately after pronouncing the name of God (in a blessing), we remember that there is no need for the blessing, we must conclude it with the verse *Lamdeni chukecha* (*Psalm 119:12*) 'Teach me Your statutes.' As this is a compete verse in itself, it is as though he had recited the Psalms, and the Name, consequently, was not mentioned in vain. If we have also begun the word *Eloheinu* (our God), but after saying *Elohei* (meaning the God of), and have not uttered the last part of the word nu (our), then we should conclude the verse *Yisrael Avinu me'olam ve'ad olam'* (*1 Chronicles 29:10*) 'Israel our Father, forever and ever.' At any rate, we are to add: 'Blessed be the name of His glorious kingdom forever and ever.'

5. If a person utters a blessing over water and then he becomes aware that someone in the neighborhood had died, when it is customary to spill out the water stored in the houses of the neighborhood,

because drinking such water is considered dangerous, he must nevertheless taste some of the water, so that his blessing shall not be uttered in vain. He need not be concerned about the danger, as the Scriptures say (*Ecclesiastes 8:5*): 'Whoso keeps the commandment shall know no evil.' After drinking a little of it, he shall spill out the rest.

6. If a person is in doubt whether he said any one of the blessings, he is not bound to repeat it, except Grace After Meals.

7. A man must pronounce at least one hundred blessings daily. This law was enacted by King David. A hint to this effect is found in the Scriptures (*II Samuel 23:1*): 'The saying of the man who was raised (In Hebrew '*Al*') on high.' The numerical value of the letters in the world *al* is one hundred. A support for this is found in the *Pentateuch* (*Deuteronomy 10:12*): 'Now O Israel, what (In Hebrew *mah*) does the Lord require of you? But to fear the Lord,' etc. Do not read *mah* (what) but *meah* (one hundred), and it refers to the one hundred blessings.' The recitation of the blessings will cause one to fear the Lord, to loving Him and to constantly remember Him. The curses contained in *Deuteronomy* (*28:15–61*) number ninety-eight, and adding to them (*loco citato 63*): 'Every sickness' and 'every plague,' the number is increased to one hundred. Now, the one hundred benedictions we utter daily, shield us from these one hundred curses. On the Sabbath, festivals and fast days, when the number of benedictions is reduced, the deficiency is filled by paying attention to the benedictions recited by the chazzan, when he repeats the *Shemoneh Esreh*, and by the blessings pronounced over the reading of the Torah and the Prophets, after which we respond *Amen*. The number may also be increased by blessings over extra dainties.

8. Upon hearing a blessing pronounced by one's fellow, one must say: *Baruch Hu uvaruch Shemo* (Blessed be He and blessed be His name) at the utterance of the Name (*Adonai*), and respond *Amen* at the conclusion of the blessing. *Amen* means it is true, and therefore when saying *Amen,* we must have in mind these two things: that what the blessing says is true, and that we believe in it

explicitly. In responding *Amen* to blessings which also include a prayer, for instance, the blessings in the *Shemoneh Esreh* beginning with *Attah chonen le'adam daat* (You favor man with knowledge) until *Hamachazir shechinato letziyon* (He who restores His divine presence to Zion) and *Sim shalom* (bestow peace), we must have in mind these two things: that the contents of the blessing is true, and that it may be the will of God that the prayer be accepted soon. In responding *Amen* to the *Kaddish,* which contains a prayer for the future only, we have in mind that the prayer be accepted soon.

9. If we are reading that portion of the prayers, during which no interruption may be made, we should not say *Baruch hu uvaruch shemo* (Blessed be He and blessed be His name). Also, when we hear a blessing to which we need only listen in order to fulfill our obligation, as for instance, the blessing said before the sounding of the *shofar,* or the reading of the *Megillah* (*Scroll of Esther*), we must not say *Baruch Hu uvaruch Shemo,* because such a response would be a break in the blessings.

The Morning Blessings

People who are in constant search of God's presence and who look for spiritual opportunities do not restrict their prayers to those taking place only within the synagogue. Rather, they tend to be duly conscious of God's role in all of their daily actions, from the moment they arise from bed in the morning until they retire for sleep at night. Those that created the prayers in the siddur were precisely that kind of people. Our great rabbis of years ago created blessings with which to praise God for life's daily wonders, many of which are often taken for granted because they occur daily and routinely.

The daily morning blessings, consisting of thanksgiving for the divine benefits bestowed upon us, were originally designed as home meditations to be recited when the Jew awakens in the morning, washes, dresses, respectively. Later on, they were included in the preliminary morning service, containing Bible and Talmud selections. The fourteenth century Abudarham mentions the blessing 'who has made me according to His will' by women in place of 'who has not made me a woman' said by men, who thank God for the privilege of performing many time bound positive mitzvot that are not incumbent upon women, owing to their manifold household duties.

BLESSING FOR WASHING HANDS:
AL NETILAT YADAYIM

The *Talmud* (*Berachot 46b*) speaks of *mayim rishonim* (washing the hands before the meal) and *mayim acharonim* (washing the hands after the meal). The very first blessing in the morning routine is for washing hands:

> Blessed are You, Lord our God, Sovereign of the Universe, who sanctified us with His commandments and commanded us concerning the washing of the hands.

The reasons for this hand washing are both for purposes of hygiene as well as a sacred act restoring one's spiritual cleanliness. It also serves as a visual reminder of the *kohen* (Jewish priest) who in Temple times would always wash his hands before offering sacrifices. Since the Jewish people are called by God in the Bible a 'kingdom of priests', washing one's hands is a way of emulating the ancient *kohanim*.

Interestingly, the Hebrew word *natal*, used in the phrase of the blessing for washing hands *netilat yadayim*, has several related meanings, so that *netilat* denotes taking, lifting up, carrying. Thus it has been suggested that the use of the expression for washing the hands implies that it is a sacred ceremony where one's hands are lifted to a higher level in order to fulfill God's commandments.

The blessing for the morning washing is properly said after dressing. Many people however recite it at the start of the morning prayers.

The religious discipline of Judaism also demands washing of the hands before eating a meal. The rabbis made a distinction between casual eating and a regular meal (*Talmud Yoma 79b*). Lest the distinction become arbitrary, they based it on the eating of bread and the recital of the prayer *hamotzi*. Bread is the staff of life, and therefore the eating of bread determined whether the meal was to be considered casual or regular. A meal at which bread is eaten must be preceded according to Jewish law by the blessing over washing the hands.

Since this washing of the hands is not a hygienic measure (because one has to wash even if one's hands are clean), but rather a religious ritual, it must be done in a specified way.

The washing should be performed with a vessel (*klee*). Thus, holding one's hands under an open faucet with the water already running is to be avoided. One typically fills a vessel with the water, holds it in one's hand, and pours it over the other, and then does the same with the second hand. After both hands are washed, the blessing is recited as the person proceeds to dry them.

Following are several other laws related to handwashing, as culled from the *Code of Jewish Law, Condensed Version:*

1. Since every man upon arising from his sleep in the morning is like a newborn creature, insofar as the worship of the Creator is concerned. He should prepare himself for worship by washing his hands out of a vessel, just as the priests used to wash their hands daily out of the wash basin before performing their service in the Temple.

   The handwashing is based on the biblical verse (*Psalms 26:6–7*): 'I will wash my hands in innocence, and I will compass Your altar, O Lord; that I may publish with a loud voice,' etc.

   There is another reason given by the Kabbalists for this morning handwashing. When a man is asleep, the holy soul departs from his body, and an unclean spirit descends upon him. When rising from sleep, the unclean spirit departs from his entire body, except from his fingers, and does not depart until one spills water upon them three times alternately. One is not allowed to walk four cubits (six feet) without having one's hands washed, except in cases of extreme necessity.

2. The ritual handwashing in the morning is performed as follows: Take a cup of water with the right hand and put it in the left; pour some water upon the right hand. Take the cup back in the right hand and pour some water on the left. This performance is repeated three times. It is best to pour the water over the hands as far as the wrists, but in case of emergency it suffices if the water covers the hands up to the joints of the fingers.

   One must also wash his face in honor of the Creator, as it is said (*Genesis 9:6*): 'For in the image of God He has made the man.' One must also rinse the mouth, because we must pronounce the Great Name in purity and cleanliness. Afterward the hands are dried.

3. The hands must be washed into a vessel only. The water thus used must not be utilized for any other purpose, because an evil spirit

rests on it (contaminated and injurious to health), and it must not be spilt in a place frequented by human beings.

4. Before the morning handwashing, one should not touch either the mouth, the nose, the eyes, the ears, the lower orifice or any kind of food, or an open vein, because the evil spirit that rests upon the hands before washing them will cause injury to these things.

5. Hands must be washed on the following occasions: On awakening from sleep, on leaving the lavatory or bath, after paring one's nails, after having one's haircut, after taking off the shoes with bare hands, after having sexual intercourse, after touching a vermin or searching the clothes for vermin, after combing one's head, after touching parts of the body which are generally covered, after leaving a cemetery, after walking in a funeral procession or leaving a house where a corpse lay, and after blood-letting.

BLESSING FOR THE GIFT OF THE BODY: *ASHER YATZAR*

Quoted in the *Talmud* (*Berachot 60b*) in the name of Abbaye, head of the school at Pumbeditha toward the end of the fourth century, the *asher yatzar* blessing refers to the complexity of the human body. It is included in the preliminary morning service as a blessing over the physical health of the worshiper. It reads:

> Praised are You, Lord our God, Sovereign of the Universe who has fashioned man in wisdom, and has created within him life sustaining organs. It is revealed and known before Your glorious throne that if but one of these functions incorrectly it would be impossible for a person to survive before You. Praised are You, O God, who endows man with health and does wonders.

This blessing praises God for creating the wondrous mechanism of the body and for preserving one's health and one's life. It clearly reflects the importance that Judaism has always attached to proper health care, and is a constant reminder that one's body belongs to God, on loan to man through his life and to be returned upon his death.

The *asher yatzar* blessing is not recited aloud by the Prayer Leader in the synagogue, but said privately by each worshiper before the start of the service. Many have the custom of reciting it after going to the bathroom. In modern times it has also been known to be recited by a person after having visited a doctor for a physical check-up and receiving a good report.

BLESSING FOR RESTORING ONE'S SOUL: *ELOHAI NESHAMAH*

After the blessing for the creation of the wondrous human body comes a blessing in which a person offers thanks to God for having created within him a pure soul that is daily restored. It reads as follows:

> O my God, the soul which You have set within me is pure. You have created it, and You did fashion it. You have breathed it into me and You have preserved it within me. You will reclaim it from me, but You will restore it to me in the life to come. So long as the breath of life is within me, I will give thanks to You, O Lord my God and God of my ancestors, Sovereign of all creation, Master of all souls. Praised are You, God, who restores life to mortal creatures.

The above blessing negates the Christian theological concept that a person is born with a tainted soul (i.e. original sin due to Adam and Eve eating of the forbidden fruit). In Judaism, all souls are born in a state of purity, and the soul of every person can be good or evil, depending on the way a person chooses to live his or her life.

The ancient rabbis also drew a parallel between death and sleep when they expressed the concept that 'sleep constitutes one sixtieth of death' (*Talmud Berachot 57b*). The prayer *Elohai Neshamah* suggests that one's daily awakening from sleep is a foreshadowing of the return and restoration of one's soul in the world to come.

THE TORAH STUDY BLESSINGS:
BIRCHOT HATORAH

It was the custom in ancient times to study some *Torah* every day before dawn, before the time of the morning prayers. That is why we find in the *siddur*, preceding the beginning of the service, several blessings on the study of *Torah*. There are three blessings because the *Talmud* records the versions preferred by different rabbis, and a later compiler of this section was apparently unwilling to choose among them.

First Blessing:

Blessed are You, O Lord our God, Sovereign of the Universe, who has sanctified us with Your precepts and commanded us to occupy ourselves with the study of the Torah.

This blessing praises God for enjoining the Jew to study Torah, one of the most critical of all mitzvot.

Second Blessing:

O Lord our God grant that we and all Your people, the House of Israel, find delight in the study of the Torah. May we and our children and all the future generations of the House of Israel know Your name and learn Your Torah for its own sake. Blessed are You, O Lord, who teaches the Torah to Your people Israel.

The second blessing praises God for giving the Jewish people the Torah. It also petitions God that Jews find delight in its many teachings.

Third Blessing:

Blessed are You, O Lord our God, Sovereign of the Universe, who has chosen us from among all peoples by giving us Your Torah. Praised are You, O God, Giver of the *Torah*.

The third blessing (also said when a person is called up for an *aliyah*) expresses thanksgiving for having been selected to receive the Torah at Mount Sinai.

Having said these three blessings on the *Torah*, one must immediately proceed to carry out the mitzvah which the blessings describe. Thus the prayer book supplies sample study passage from the *Bible*, *Mishnah*, and the *Talmud* so that every person can study at least a little *Torah* every day. This begins a pattern of the Jewish liturgy which interweaves prayer and various forms of study.

In the first study section presented in the prayer book, the Bible passage consists of the verses of the Priestly Blessing (*Numbers 6:24–26*).

The *Mishnah* selection is from the tractate of *Peah 1:1*:

> These are the obligations for which no fixed measure is imposed: leaving the corner of the field for the poor, the gift of the first fruits, the pilgrimage offering, deeds of kindness and study of the Torah.

The *Gemara* selection is excerpted from the Talmudic tractate of *Shabbat 127a*:

> These are the commandments the fruits of which a person enjoys in this world while the principal remains for him to enjoy in the world to come: They are: honoring father and mother, deeds of kindness, early attendance, morning and evening at the house of study... But the study of *Torah* is basic to them all.

THE FIFTEEN MORNING BLESSINGS

The ancient rabbis have suggested that Jews should begin their worship service praising God (*Talmud Berachot 32a*). Most congregations follow the practice of beginning the daily morning service with the series of blessings said upon arising. Collectively, these blessings are known as *birchot hashachar*.

The *Talmud* (*Berachot 60b*) lists a series of blessings that a person is to say when arising. Each blessing opens with the traditional standard formula 'Blessed are You, Lord our God, Sovereign of the Universe, and concludes as follows:

> …who has given the rooster the wisdom to distinguish between day and night
> …who has made me in God's image
> …who made me a Jew
> …who made me free
> …who opens the eyes of the blind
> …who clothes the unclothed
> …who frees the bound
> …who helps those who are bent over by trouble stand straight
> …who spreads out the earth over the waters
> …who made for me everything I need
> …who prepares the way for our footsteps
> …who gives the people of Israel strength
> …who crowns the people of Israel with glory
> …who gives strength to the weary

Each of these blessings are connected to the orderly routine when one awakens in the morning. The blessings begin with the act of awakening itself, then move on to the dressing of the body and finally to the act removing slumber from one's eyelids.

- The first blessing has its biblical origins in the *Book of Job 38:36*. The rooster was originally God's wake-up call when the Jewish people were an agricultural society.
- The opening of the eyes blessing expresses gratitude to God for giving us wisdom and understanding.
- To be able to stand tall and erect and sure footed on the ground is also a blessing for which the Jew expresses gratitude each and every day.
- The blessing 'who clothes the unclothed' is an allusion to God having clothed the first human beings, Adam and Eve. (*Genesis 3:7*). It is also a reminder of the Jew's responsibility to see to it that

all people who lack clothing be given assistance. Interestingly, this blessing is also recited when putting on a new garment.

- God's care for His creatures is manifested in the blessings 'who made for me everything I need' and 'who prepares the way of our footsteps.' Several commentators have posited that the latter blessing was to be said in conjunction with putting on one's shoes, symbolizing an important necessity.
- The blessing 'who gives the people of Israel strength' was often associated with putting on a waist belt, the symbol of strength in ancient times. It was on the waist belt that a person kept his weapons.
- The blessing 'who crowns the people of Israel with glory' was customarily associated with putting on one's headgear as a sign of respect to God.

Thus the total of fifteen morning blessings thank God for giving a person all of one's necessities with which to move on with one's day. Giving gratitude to God for His many kindnesses by reciting daily blessings becomes a special means for communion between man and God, elevating even those most routine acts into the realm of the spiritual.

Rabbi Reuven Kimelman writes in his article 'The Blessings of Prayerobics' that we need movement in prayer, today often referred to as 'embodied prayer.' That is to say, we need to combine prayer with physical actions in order for praying to be a more spiritual experience. He calls these prayer movements 'prayerobics.' Following are some of his suggestions when reciting the blessings of the morning:

- For the prayer 'Praised are You, God, who opens the eyes of the blind,' rub your eyes, and open them wide to see the dawning of a new day.
- For 'Praised are You, God, who prepares the way for our footsteps,' take your first step, and then chant the blessing.
- For 'Praised are You, God, who clothes the unclothed,' stroke your clothes and feel the warmth of God's caring. Then chant the blessing.

- For 'Praised are You, God, who frees the bound,' stretch your arms, breathe deeply, expand your chest, and recite the blessing.
- For 'Praised are You, God, who raises those who are bowed down,' spring erect from a bent position, arch your spine, and look heavenward. Then chant the blessing.
- For 'Praised are You, God, who removes sleep from my eyes,' massage your face and close your eyes and massage them. Open your eyes carefully and wipe their corners, removing the 'slumber particles.' Then chant the final blessing.

LAWS OF THE MORNING BLESSINGS

Following is a summary of the laws of the morning blessings as culled from the *Code of Jewish Law, Condensed Version*.

- The blessing 'who gives the rooster understanding...' should not be uttered before daylight.
- The blessing 'who opens the eyes of the blind' may be said even by a blind person, for he too, benefitted by sight, in that others can show him the way. If one happens to say the blessing 'who raises the bowed down' before the blessing 'who sets the captives free', that is, loosens the joints of one's body to give one free movement and co-ordination of muscles, one need not repeat the latter, as it has already been covered by the former.
- Even if one is awake all night one must say the morning blessings, except the blessing concerning the washing of the hands. It is doubtful whether or not he has to say the blessings, *Elohai neshamah* (my God, the soul, *etc.*), and *hama'avir shenah* (He who takes sleep away). It is also doubtful whether he should say the blessing over the Law. It is, therefore, good practice to hear others say these blessings and respond Amen to them.
- If one has not said the morning blessings before praying, he must say them after that, except the blessing *al netilat yadayim* (for some authorities hold that the washing of the hands in the morning was ordained primarily because of the prayers), but when the praying is done already, there is no longer any need for this blessing.

The *Shema* and its Blessings

The *Shema* prayer was recited publicly after the Ten Commandments in the Temple service. Later, by the first century of the common era, the three paragraphs constituting the *Shema* became the core of the synagogue service, along with the *Amidah*.

Recited as the confession of the Jewish faith, the opening verse of the *Shema* (*Deuteronomy 6:4*) sums up the first and second commandments of the Ten Commandments: Hear O Israel, the Lord our God, the Lord is One. The *Mishnah* (*Berachot 2:5*) refers to the reciting of the *Shema* as the acceptance of the yoke of the divine majesty. The *Shema* was ever on the lips of Jewish martyrs. Rabbi Akiva endured the greatest tortures while his flesh was being born with iron combs and died pronouncing the word *echad* (one) with his last breath.

Today, the *Shema Yisrael* is the password by which Jews recognize one another throughout the world. It has been asserted that anyone who has not seen a Jew say *Shema* at the *Neila* service at the end of the Day of Atonement or the confession before death has never seen religious ecstasy.

Since it is a religious obligation to recite the *Shema* it should come as no surprise that the sages of old would have required the worshipper to preface its performance with the reciting of a blessing. As a matter of fact, there are also prescribed blessings to be recited after the *Shema* as well. The *Mishnah* (*Berachot 1:4*) rules: 'In the morning one recites two blessings before and two after.'

The blessings that bracket the *Shema* on either end emphasize God as the creator of the world, God's everlasting love for the people of Israel and God as Redeemer of the Israelites. The blessings before serve as stepping stones to the *Shema's* declaration of faith in One God, while the blessings after the Shema refer to the anticipated result of such faith.

Here now is a summary of the blessings before and after the Shema.

FIRST BLESSING BEFORE THE MORNING *SHEMA*

The first blessing before the *Shema* is called *Birkat HaYotzer* – 'The Blessing of Creation.' The first sentence of the blessing is based on *Isaiah 45:7*, which ends with the word evil. However, the Rabbis changed the word *ra* (evil) to the word *hakol* (all things), thus stressing the compassionate side of God. Some commentators have also asserted that the blessing serves as a polemic against the Persian belief in dualism, in which Ahuramazda was the god of light and goodness while Ahriman was the god of darkness and evil. Thus, to combat the idea that the god who created darkness would not also create light, the rabbis ordained the blessing in the present form. Following are excerpts from the first blessing before the *Shema*:

> Praised are You, Lord our God, Sovereign of the universe, who forms light and creates darkness, who makes peace and creates all things. Who mercifully casts light upon the earth and upon all who live thereon. And in whose goodness renews the works of creation each day continually. How manifold are Your works, O God, in wisdom You have made them all, the earth is filled with all of Your creations…God is the Lord of wonders, who in His goodness renews the work of creation every day continually. As it is said, Give thanks to God who makes great lights, for His kindness endures eternally. Cause a new light to shine upon Zion and may we all be worthy to soon enjoy its brightness. Praised are You, Lord, Creator of lights.

FIRST BLESSING BEFORE THE EVENING *SHEMA*

The first blessing before the evening *Shema* is called *Birkat Maariv* – Evening Blessing. The evening service equivalent of the *Birkat HaYotzer* cited above is the prayer which immediately follows the *Barechu*, the call to worship. The concepts in the first blessing of the evening *Shema* are similar to those of the morning blessing. The basic idea of the first blessing of the evening *Shema* is that one God rules over all, and has the capacity to create and bring both day and night and the regular changes in time and season. Knowing this is a source of comfort to the worshiper.

Following is the first blessing before the evening Shema:

> Praised are You, Lord our God, Ruler of the universe, whose word brings the evening dusk. With wisdom God opens the gates of the heavens, changes the times of day with understanding, exchanges the season, and puts the stars in their proper place and order in the sky. Creator of day and night, rolling the light away before the darkness and the darkness before the light. God causes the day to pass and brings night, separating between day and night –*Adonai Tzeva'ot* is God's name. The God who lives forever will rule over us forever and ever. Praised are You, Lord, who brings the evening dusk.

SECOND BLESSING BEFORE THE MORNING *SHEMA*

The second blessing before the morning *Shema* is called *Ahavah Rabbah* (with great love). It serves as a kind of *Torah* blessing for the *Shema* which follows immediately after it. The concepts of this blessing include the following:

- God shows His love for the Israelites by giving them the Torah.
- God is both Father and Sovereign
- We petition God to teach us to understand, learn, teach, and observe His law.
- At the end of *Ahavah Rabbah* we have the concept of the ingathering of the exiles from the four corners of the earth. (Symbolically, every worshipper wearing a *tallit* customarily gathers the four fringes of his or her prayer shawl, symbolic of the coming together of all the Jews from the four corners of the world).
- God chooses His people Israel with love.

Here are the words of the second blessing of the morning Shema:

> With great love have You loved us, Lord our God. With great and extra tenderness You have cared for us. Our Parent, our Ruler, for the sake of our ancestors who trusted in You, and who taught life-giving laws, be kind to us, too, and teach us. Our merciful Parent treat us with mercy, and help our minds to understand Your Torah, teaching us to listen, to learn and to teach, to observe, to do, and to fulfill all its words with love. Light up our eyes with Your *Torah* and cause our hearts to hold tight to Your commandments. Unify our hearts to love and respect Your name so that we will never be ashamed. For we trust in Your holy, great, and awe-inspiring name. May we rejoice in Your saving power. Gather us in peace from the four corners of the earth, and lead us to our land with our heads held high, for You are a God who is able to rescue. You have chosen us from all peoples and brought us near to You, to thank You sincerely and to announce with love that You are One. Praised are You, God, who lovingly chooses the people of Israel.

SECOND BLESSING BEFORE THE EVENING SHEMA

The second blessing before the evening *Shema* is called *Ahavat Olam* (everlasting love). Interestingly, the Sephardic and Italian rituals use only *Ahavat Olam* both morning and evening. Analogous to the *Ahavah Rabbah* blessing before the morning *Shema*, its concepts include love of Israel, happiness with the words of *Torah*, a desire to meditate about the *Torah's* words both day and night and praising God for loving the Israelites.

Following are the words of the *Ahavat Olam*:

> You have always loved Your people Israel by teaching us *Torah*, *mitzvot*, laws and justice. Therefore, Lord our God, when we lie down at night and when we get up in the morning, we will talk about Your laws. We will always be happy with the words of Your *Torah* and Your commandments because they are our life, and they give long life. We will think about them day and night. May

You never take Your love away from us. Praised are You, God, who loves the people Israel.

BLESSING AFTER THE MORNING
AND EVENING *SHEMA*

The blessing after the *Shema,* both at the morning and evening service, acknowledges God's deliverance of the children of Israel from Egyptian bondage. It is called the *Birkat Ge'ulah* --the blessing of Redemption, and includes these two famous biblical passages that are part of the Song of Moses (*i.e.,* the song which Moses and the children of Israel sang when they crossed the Red Sea). The blessing's main theme is the redemption of Israel from Egypt and the dependability and reliability that God will continue to help the Israelites in wondrous ways in the future as well. Here are the words to the biblical passages from the Song of Moses:

> Who is like You, O God, among the mighty?
> Who is like You, magnificent in holiness, awesome in praises, doing
> wonders? (*Exodus 15:11*)

We also repeat the proclamation that the children of Israel said at that time:

> The Lord shall reign for ever and ever. (*Exodus 15:18*)

The expression 'Rock of Israel' (*Tzur Yisrael*), a reference to God in the last paragraph of this blessing said in the morning, is taken from the *Book of Isaiah 30:29.* The same phrase was incorporated into the *State of Israel's Declaration of Independence,* signed on May 14, 1948:

'With trust in the Rock of Israel, we affix our signatures in testimony to this declaration.'

FIRST BLESSING AFTER THE EVENING *SHEMA*:
BIRKAT GEULAH – BLESSING OF REDEMPTION

Unlike the morning *Shema*, the evening *Shema* is followed by two blessings. The first one has as its theme praise of God for Redeeming the Israelites. God is referred to as having no peer or equal. God is also described as intimate, close, and approachable:

> We affirm the truth that He is our God, that there is no other, and that we are His people Israel. God redeems us from the power of Sovereigns, delivers us from the hand of all tyrants. God brings judgment upon all our oppressors, retribution upon all our mortal enemies…
>
> Thus it is written: 'The Lord has rescued Jacob. God redeemed him from those more powerful.' Praised are You, God, Redeemer of the Israelites.

SECOND BLESSING AFTER THE EVENING *SHEMA*:
HASHKIVEINU – BLESSING ON RETIRING

The second blessing after the evening *Shema* praises God for His protecting care at night. The night is a time when a person especially feels the need of God's watchfulness over him. Living in Babylonia during Talmudic times was especially dangerous at nighttime, when criminals roamed the rural roads with great frequency.

The *Midrash* on *Psalm 6* tells us that this blessing comes to replace the obligation of *tzitzit* (fringes), which is not observed at night. As the worshipper is reminded in the day by the fringes of the prayer shawl to follow God's *mitzvot*, at night we challenge God to protect us beneath His wings so we can continue to follow those laws and have hope for the future. Here are the words of the second blessing after the evening *Shema*:

> Cause us O Lord our God to lie down in peace, and raise us up O our Sovereign to life. Spread over us the protection of Your peace. Direct us aright through Your good counsel. Save us for

Your Name's sake. Be a shield about us. Remove from us every foe, pestilence, sword, famine, and sorrow. Also remove the adversary from before us and from behind us. Shelter us beneath the shadow of Your wings. You, O God are guardian and deliverer. You are a gracious and merciful Sovereign. Guard our coming and our going unto life and peace from this time forth and forever more. Praised are You, O Lord, who guards your people Israel forever.

The Shabbat version of this prayer ends with the phrase 'who spreads the Sukkah of peace over us, over Israel and over Jerusalem.'

The Blessings of the *Amidah*

The *Amidah* prayer is alternatively known as the *Shemoneh Esrai* (Eighteen) or *Hatefillah* (The Prayer). It is called the *Shemoneh Esrai* because it was originally composed of eighteen different blessings. It is also called *Hatefillah* because it was considered the heart of Jewish worship.

According to tradition, the *Amidah* and its blessings were composed by Members of the Great Assembly who flourished at the early period of the Second Temple. Shortly after the destruction of the Second Temple in the first century of the Common Era, the form and order of the *Amidah* blessings were crystallized by Simon Ha-Pakuli in Yavneh at the request of Rabbi Gamaliel (*Talmud Megillah 17b*).

Originally, the *Amidah* consisted of eighteen blessings. In its present form, however, there are nineteen blessings. The addition of the paragraph concerning the slanderers and enemies of the people was made toward the end of the first century at the direction of Rabban Gamaliel 11, head of the *Sanhedrin* at Yavneh.

The *Talmud* offers a variety of reasons for the original number of eighteen. It corresponds to the eighteen times that God is mentioned in *Psalm 29* as well as in the *Shema*. The three patriarchs of the Jewish people, Abraham, Isaac, and Jacob are mentioned together eighteen times in the Hebrew Bible. The number eighteen is also said to correspond to the eighteen vertebrae of the spinal column (*Talmud Berachot 28b*).

The *Shemoneh Esrai* is now generally referred to as the *Amidah* (standing) because it is recited in a standing posture. On the Sabbaths and on Festivals, the first three blessings and the last three are the same in all forms of the *Amidah*. The thirteen blessings of the weekday *Amidah* are eliminated on the grounds that no personal requests may be made during Sabbaths and Festivals. Upon reciting these petitions, a person is reminded of his failings and troubles, and on the days of rest one ought to be cheerful and not saddened by worries.

The middle paragraphs of the weekday *Amidah* contain petitions for the fulfillment of a person's needs. They plead for wisdom, repentance, forgiveness, deliverance, healing, prosperity, ingathering of the exiled, restoration of justice, suppression of tyranny, protection of the upright, rebuilding of Jerusalem, the messianic era, and the acceptance of prayer. All of these petitions are recited on behalf of the entire community.

LAWS AND CUSTOMS RELATED TO THE *AMIDAH*

As with all prayers, the *Amidah* is recited while facing east (toward the city of Jerusalem). Worshipers in Jerusalem face towards the Temple Mount, where the Temple once stood.

The proper worshiper etiquette while reciting the *Amidah* is to have one's feet together at attention. (A biblical inference for this custom can be found in the *Book of Ezekiel 1:7*: 'And their feet were as a straight foot.') This is generally interpreted to mean that the angels' feet in Ezekiel's vision appeared as one foot. (*Talmud Berachot 10b*) Thus, when one communicates with God, one should take a similar position to that of God's ministering angels.

In traditional settings the *Amidah* is first said silently by all of the worshippers and then repeated aloud by the Prayer Leader. This is based on the example of the prophet Samuel's mother Hannah who in the *First Book of Samuel 1:13* is described as 'speaking in her heart, with her lips moving but her voice not being heard.'

The custom before beginning the *Amidah* itself is for the worshiper to take three small steps. Where space is limited the practice is to move back several small steps before taking the first three steps forward. This procedure was analogous to the procedure when a servant of a King would approach His majesty. Similarly, one is to approach the 'King of Kings' in the same manner.

At the end of the *Amidah* while reciting the sentence *oseh shalom bimromav* (May God who establishes peace) the custom is to slightly bow three times from the waist, first towards the left, then towards the right, and then forward. This is analogous to the way in which a subject took leave of his King.

The custom of repeating the *Amidah* aloud at both the morning *Shacharit* and afternoon *Mincha* services is for the benefit of those who were not able to recite it properly. By listening carefully and answering *Amen* at the right places all worshipers can properly fulfill their obligation.

Following are several other laws related to the recitation of the *Amidah* as culled from the *Code of Jewish Law, Condensed Version*.

- When reciting the *Shemoneh Esrai*, the worshiper should always be mindful of the fact that the Divine Presence is before him, as it is written (*Lamentations 2:19*): 'Pour out your heart like water before the face of the Lord.' He should concentrate on the prayers, and banish from his mind all thoughts that may trouble him. Let him think: if he were to speak to a mortal king, he would properly prepare his speech and take care not to blunder. How much more, should he concentrate his thoughts when speaking to the Supreme King of kings, blessed be He, because to Him, blessed be His name, thoughts are like spoken words, and He examines all thoughts. Before praying, he should think of the majesty of God, blessed be His name, and of the low state of man, and banish from his mind all thoughts of human pleasures.
- The worshiper should place his feet close together as if they were but one, simulating the angels, of whom it is written (*Ezekiel 1:7*): 'And their feet were straight feet,' that is, their feet appeared as though they were one foot. He should droop his head slightly, and close his eyes as not to look at anything. And if he reads from a Siddur, he should not take his eyes off the book. He should place his hands over his heart, the right hand over the left, and

pray wholeheartedly, with fear and reverence and humility in the manner of a poor man standing at the door begging for alms, and he should pronounce the words feelingly and correctly. Everyone should read the prayers according to his own text, whether it be Ashkenazic or Sephardic; they are both of sacred origin. But one must not confuse the texts, because the words of each text are numbered and in accordance with profound mystic speculations, and nothing should be either added or subtracted.

• One should be careful to read the *Shemoneh Esrai* quietly, so that only he himself may hear what he says, but not the one standing next to him, as it is written of Hannah (*1 Samuel 1:13*): 'Only her lips moved, but her voice could not be heard.'

• One should not lean against anything while praying the *Shemoneh Esrei*, unless one is ill, in which case he may read it sitting or even lying down, provided that he concentrates his thoughts upon the prayers. If he is too ill to articulate the words, he should meditate the prayers in his heart.

• When praying the *Shemoneh Esrai*, one must not belch, or stretch, or yawn. If he must do so, he should place his hand over his mouth, and cover it. He must not spit or expectorate, but if there is saliva in his mouth and he is annoyed by it to the extent that he cannot concentrate on the prayer, he should eject it in a handkerchief. And if this is loathsome to him, he should turn to the left and expectorate on his left side. If he cannot do it on the left, he may then do it on the right.

• When praying the *Shemoneh Esrai*, we must stand facing the Land of Israel, as it is written (*1 Kings 8:48*): 'And they pray to You toward their land.' We should also face Jerusalem, the Holy Temple, and the Holy of Holies. Therefore, we who dwell west of the land of Israel turn toward the east (not exactly east, but southeast). People living north of the land of Israel turn towards the south. Those living east turn toward the west, and those living south turn toward the north. Thus all Israelites turn their faces towards one place, namely towards Jerusalem and the Holy of Holies.

- It is necessary to bend the knees and bow four times while saying the *Shemoneh Esrei*, at the beginning and at the end of the first blessing, at the beginning and the end of the blessing *Modim* (we give thanks). When we say *baruch* (blessed are) we bend the knees, and then we say *Ata* (You) we bow, so that the vertebrae of the spinal column protrude, and we also bow our heads. Before pronouncing the Name (*Adonai*) we slowly raise ourselves to an erect position, for it is written (*Psalm 148:8*): 'The Lord raises up them that are bowed down.' So at *Modim,* we bend the knees and bow, and before uttering the name of God, we straighten up. We must not bow down too much, so that the mouth be opposite the girdle, because this is an act of ostentation. Old people and invalids, to whom bending the knees is painful, should merely incline their heads. Additional genuflections for the other blessings, either at their beginning or their end are forbidden.

- On concluding the *Shemoneh Esrai*, we recite *Elohai netzor* (O God, guard), and before saying *Oseh Shalom* (He who makes peace), we should bow and walk only three steps backward after the manner of a servant who takes leave of his master. The steps should be of average size, the minimum of which is that the toe should touch the heel. While still bowed, we should turn our face toward the left, which is the right of the Divine Presence, who is before us while we are praying. Upon concluding our prayer we should say: *Oseh shalom bimromav* (He who makes peace in the high places). And we turn our face towards our right, which is towards the left of the Divine Presence, and we say: *Hu yaaseh shalom alenu* (May He make peace for us). Thereafter, we bow towards the front, and say: *Ve'al kol yisrael veimreru amen.* (And for all Israel, and say ye Amen).

- While saying the *Shemoneh Esrai* the worshiper should not blink his eyes, nor twitch his lips, nor point his finger, nor interrupt for the *kaddish, kedushah* or *barechu.* He must remain silent and pay attention to what the hazan and the congregation are saying, and this will be accounted to him as if he had actually participated in the response of the congregation, albeit not considered an interruption.

- If a person feels the slightest need to respond to the call of nature, he is not allowed to begin his prayers until he does so. So much more so, a person is forbidden to commence the *Shemoneh Esrai* if he has the slightest feeling that he needs to respond to the call of nature.
- A feeble person should not be prevented from remaining seated within four cubits of one praying the *Shemoneh Esrai*.
- It is forbidden to pass within four cubits in front of one praying the *Shemoneh Esreh*. Therefore, if one concludes his prayer and the one standing behind him is still praying, the former must step backward the required three steps, because it is equivalent to passing in front of a praying man. It is permissible, however, to pass at his side and certainly behind him.
- If a person is intoxicated to the extent that he would not be able to speak with the deference due a great and respected person, he is not permitted to say the *Shemoneh Esrai*. If a man does the *Shemoneh Esrai* in such a condition, his prayer is considered an abomination and he is obliged to repeat the prayer when he is sober.

THE STRUCTURE OF THE *AMIDAH*

The *Amidah* blessings follow a logical structure. The logic underlying the structure of the *Amidah* is expressed in the *Talmud* as follows:

Rav Yehudah said, 'One should never request his needs in the first three blessings or in the last three, but only in the middle ones,' since Rabbi Hanina said, 'The first section – like a servant who organizes his praise of his master; the middle – like a servant requesting a payment from his master. The end – like a servant who received payment from his master and takes his leave.'

Following is a summary chart outlining the basic structure of the weekday *Amidah* and its blessings:

Order and Name of Blessing	Beginning Words
PRAISE OF GOD	
1. *Avot* (Ancestors)	*Baruch ata*
2. *Gevurot* (Power of God)	*Atah gibor*
3. *Kedushah* (Holiness of God)	*Atah kadosh*
4. *Binah* (Knowledge)	*Atah chonen*
Spiritual Needs	
5. *Teshuvah* (Repentance)	*Hasheevaynu*
6. *Selichah* (Forgiveness)	*Selach Lanu*
7. *Geulah* (Redemption)	*Re'eh v'onyeinu*
PERSONAL PHYSICAL NEEDS	
8. *Refu'ah* (Health)	*Refaeinu*
9. *Birkat Hashanim* (Economic prosperity)	*Bareich aleinu*
NATIONAL PHYSICAL NEEDS	
10. *Kibbutz Galuyot* (Ingathering of exiles)	*Teka bashofar*
11. *Birkat Hamishpat* (Restoration of Justice)	*Hashiva shofeteinu*
12. *Birkat Haminim* (Destruction of Israel's Enemies	*V'lamalshinim*
13. *Birkat Hatzaddikim* (Prayer for the Righteous)	*Al haTzaddikim*
14. *Birkat Yerushalayim* (Restoration of Jerusalem)	*V'al Yerushalayim*
15. *Birkat David* (Coming of the Messiah)	*Et tzemach David*
16. *Tefillah* (Hear our prayer)	*Shema Koleinu*
THANKING GOD	
17. *Avodah* (Worship)	*Retzei*
18. *Birkat Hoda'ah* (Thanksgiving)	*Modim*
19. *Birkat Shalom* (Peace)	*Sim Shalom*

The Introductory Three Blessings

FIRST BLESSING: *AVOT* (ANCESTORS)

The first blessing describes God as the God of our ancestors Abraham, Isaac, and Jacob.

> Praised are You, Lord our God and God of our ancestors, God of Abraham, God of Isaac, and God of Jacob. The great, mighty, and awesome God, God on high. You act with lovingkindness and create everything. God remembers the loving deeds of our ancestors, and will bring a redeemer to their children's children because that is God's loving nature. You are a helping, saving, and shielding Ruler. Praised are You, God, shield of Abraham.

As God was their protector, so too will He continue to be the protector of the Jewish family. God is also described as remembering the good deeds of the patriarchs. This concept in Jewish theology is expressive of the idea that the Jewish people will profit in their lifetime because of the multitude of meritorious acts of their ancestors. (*Note*: During the Ten Days of Penitence the refrain *zachreynu lechayim* – remember us for life is added, which furthers the appeal to God, who desires life, to protect the Israelites with life).

SECOND BLESSING: *GEVUROT* (POWER)

The next blessing praises God's amazing ability to perform wondrous works:

> You are mighty forever, O God. You give life to the dead with Your great saving power. You support the living with kindness. You give

life to the dead with great mercy. You support the fallen, heal the sick, and set free those in prison. You keep faith with those who sleep in the dust. Who is like You, Mighty Ruler, and who can compare to You? You are the Ruler of life and death and causes salvation to bloom. You are trustworthy in giving life to the dead. Praised are You, who gives life to the dead.

In the second blessing of the *Amidah* we see that God's power is so great that it is even able to revive the dead. Three times in the second blessing there is a reference to God's ability to make the dead come to life. This emphasis reflects an old controversy with the Samaritans, which was later taken up by the Sadducees and others, who denied this belief.

The precise meaning of God's revivification of the dead is still under much debate. The commentator Nachmanides interpreted it literally as the eternal resurrection of the body in this world. Maimonides regarded it as a sort of second chance normal life that would only be temporary.

THIRD BLESSING: *KEDUSHAT HASHEM* (HOLINESS OF GOD)

The third blessing of the *Amidah* focuses on the theme of God's holiness.

You are holy and Your name is holy; And those who are holy shall praise You every day. Praised are You, Lord, the Holy God.

When the *Amidah* is repeated after the Prayer Leader, the congregation rises immediately following the second blessing to say the prayer known as the *Kedushah* (Sanctification), which serves as an introduction to the third *Amidah* blessing. The *Kedushah* is based on biblical passages from *Isaiah 6:3, Ezekiel 3:12* and *Psalms 146:10*.

The Middle Thirteen Blessings: Petitioning God

FOURTH BLESSING: *BINAH* (KNOWLEDGE)

The *Amidah's* fourth blessing reads as follows:

> You grant knowledge to people and teach understanding to human beings. Grant us knowledge, discernment, and wisdom. Praised are You, God, who grants intelligence.

The fourth, fifth and sixth blessings deal with the spiritual needs of the worshipper. The fourth blessing is the first petition by the worshiper, asking for knowledge and understanding, in order to know how to use God's blessings and gifts. Interestingly, when King Solomon was asked by God to make a wish in a dream, Solomon asked for wisdom and knowledge (*II Chronicles 1:10*).

FIFTH BLESSING: *TESHUVAH* (REPENTANCE)

When one knows how to reason, one can then be fully responsible for one's actions. The fifth blessing of the *Amidah* petitions God to have our repentance accepted. It reads as follows:

> Our Father bring us back to Your Torah. Our Sovereign draw us near to Your service. Lead us back to You, truly repentant. Praised are You, God, who welcomes repentance.

SIXTH BLESSING: *SELICHAH* (FORGIVENESS)

In the sixth blessing the worshiper petitions God to be accepting of his or her forgiveness:

Forgive us, O our Father, for we have sinned; Pardon us, Sovereign One, for we have transgressed; For You do pardon and forgive. Praised are You, God, who is gracious and does abundantly forgive.

SEVENTH BLESSING: *GEULAH* (REDEMPTION)

The seventh *Amidah* blessing petitions God to redeem the worshiper from affliction and oppression:

Look upon our affliction and plead our cause, and redeem us speedily for your Name's sake. For you are a mighty Redeemer. Praised are You, O God, the Redeemer of Israel.

EIGHTH BLESSING: *REFUAH* (HEALING)

The eighth *Amidah* blessing is a petition for healing of all who are sick, strength for all who are weak, and relief for all who suffer pain:

Heal us, O God, and we shall be healed. Save us and we shall be saved. For You are our praise. Grant a perfect healing to our wounds, for You, Almighty Sovereign, are a faithful and merciful Physician. Praised are You, O God, who heals the sick of your people Israel.

Personal prayers for a sick relative or friend are traditionally added as part of this blessing.

NINTH BLESSING: *BIRKAT HASHANIM* (ECONOMIC PROSPERITY)

Economic security is an especially important component of one's physical and mental well-being. This blessing was created at the time in which the Jewish people were an agricultural society.

Bless this year unto us, O God, together with every kind of produce thereof, for our welfare. Provide dew and rain as a blessing on the face of the earth. Satisfy us with Your goodness and bless our year like other good years. Praised are You, O God, who blesses the years.

TENTH BLESSING: *KIBBUTZ GALUYOT* (INGATHERING OF EXILES)

Long before the destruction of the Jewish State, there was a widespread Jewish dispersion in Mediterranean lands, in Babylonia and in the neighboring countries. The tenth *Amidah* blessing petitions God that the people of Israel be gathered together in their homeland:

> Sound the great horn for our freedom. Raise the ensign to gather our exiles, and gather us from the four corners of earth. Blessed are You, O God, who gathers the dispersed of your people Israel.

ELEVENTH BLESSING: *TZEDAKAH U'MISHPAT* (RESTORATION OF JUSTICE)

Self-rule and the ability to establish Jewish leadership and the right to self-determination in our own land underlie this blessing. It was developed when Jews were not in control of their own destiny:

> Restore our judges as in former times, and our counsellors as at the beginning. Remove from us sorrow and sighing. Reign over us, O God, You alone, in lovingkindness and tender mercy, and clear us in judgment. Praised are You, O God, the Sovereign who loves righteousness and judgment.

TWELFTH BLESSING: *MINIM* (DESTRUCTION OF ISRAEL'S ENEMIES)

This petition is an addition to the eighteen blessings of the *Amidah*, which by it became nineteen. It is directed against Jewish sectaries (*minim*) in the generation after the destruction of the Second Temple. They caused much division in the religious camp of Israel.

> And for slanderers, let there be no hope, and let all wickedness perish as in a moment. Let all your enemies be speedily cut off, and the dominion of arrogance do you uproot and crush. Cast down and humble speedily in our days. Praised are You, O God, who breaks the enemies and humbles the arrogant.

THIRTEENTH BLESSING: *TZADDIKIM*
(PRAYER FOR THE RIGHTEOUS)

This blessing petitions God to reward the righteous and the saintly and to make their presence felt. Righteous non-Jews will also have a place in that society.

> Towards the righteous and the pious, towards the elders of your people the house of Israel, towards the remnant of their scribes, towards proselytes, and towards us also may your tender mercies be stirred, O Lord our God. Grant a good reward to all who faithfully trust in your name. Set our portion with them forever, so that we may not be put to shame. For we have trusted in you. Praised are You, O God, the stay and trust of the righteous.

FOURTEENTH BLESSING:
YERUSHALAYIM (JERUSALEM)

The rebuilding of Jerusalem as the city of righteousness would usher in the Messianic era. This blessing petitions God to dwell in the Land of Israel, with Jerusalem as its capital.

> And to Jerusalem, Your city, return in mercy, and dwell therein as You have spoken. Rebuild it soon in our days as an everlasting building, and speedily set up therein the throne of David. Praised are You, God, who rebuilds Jerusalem.

FIFTEENTH BLESSING: *BIRKAT DAVID*
(COMING OF THE MESSIAH)

According to Jewish tradition, the Messiah will be a descendant of the royal House of David. When all the previously national requests in the *Amidah* blessings of petition are granted, salvation will come and the messianic age will arrive.

> Speedily cause the offspring of David, your servant, to flourish, and lift up his glory by your Divine help because we wait for your

salvation all through the day. Praised are You O God who causes the strength of salvation to flourish.

This blessing about the Messiah's coming and the one preceding about the restoration of Jerusalem were originally one blessing that concluded with the words: 'God of David and Builder of Jerusalem', or according to another version, 'Builder of Jerusalem and Savior of Israel.' The fifteenth blessing concludes the series of blessing that relate to the redemption of the Israelites.

SIXTEENTH BLESSING: *SHOME'A TEFILLAH* (HEAR OUR PRAYER)

This is the final petition: that God hear and accept our prayers. A version of this prayer was once said by the High Priest in Temple times. It is also customary for a worshipper to add his or her own private petitions and requests here. Following are the words of the sixteenth blessing:

> Hear our voice, O Lord our God; spare us and have mercy upon us, and accept our prayer in mercy and favor. For you are a God who listens to prayers and supplications. From Your presence, O our Sovereign, turn us not away empty, for You listen in mercy to the prayer of Your people Israel. Praised are You, O Lord, who listens to prayers.

The Concluding Three Blessings: Thanking God

The last section of the *Amidah* consists of three blessings that are the same in every *Amidah* throughout the year. These three blessings constitute a unit in which we petition God to receive our prayer offering, we thank God for past, present and future kindnesses, and we pray for peace.

SEVENTEENTH BLESSING: *AVODAH* (WORSHIP)

In this blessing we petition God to receive with love our prayer offerings. Originally recited by the priest at the end of the Temple service, this section came to be a reminder of the special form of worship in the Temple and the hope that Zion would always remain the center of the Jewish spiritual world.

> Accept, O Lord our God, your people Israel and their prayer; restore the service to the inner sanctuary of your house; receive in love and favor both the offerings of Israel and their prayer. And may the worship of your people Israel be ever acceptable unto you.

EIGHTEENTH BLESSING: *HODA'AH* (THANKSGIVING)

This section was originally recited after the sacrifice in the Temple, when people bowed down on the floor. Today the custom is to bow at the beginning and end of this blessing, which is introduced by a phrase from *1 Chronicles 29:13*, *Modim anachnu lach*, stating our gratitude to God. In this section we thank God for the daily miracles of life.

> We give thanks to you, for You are the Lord our God and God of our fathers for ever and ever. You are the Rock of our lives, the Shield of our salvation through every generation. We will give thanks to You and declare Your praise for our lives which are committed unto Your hand, and for our souls which are in Your charge, and for Your miracles which are daily with us, and for Your wonders and Your benefits, which are brought at all times, evening, morn, and noon. O You who are all good, whose mercies fail not; You who are merciful, whose kindness never ceases, we have ever hoped in You. Everything that lives shall give thanks to you forever, and shall praise Your name in truth, O God, our salvation and help. Praised are You, O Lord, whose Name is all good and unto whom it is becoming to give thanks.

NINETEENTH BLESSING: *SHALOM* (PEACE)

The Priestly Blessing (*Numbers 6:24–26*) is added here as a prelude to the closing nineteenth blessing when the *Amidah* is repeated. The blessing was probably inserted here because it is reminiscent of the Temple service, seen in the *Avodah* section. Jewish tradition considers peace to be the greatest blessing of them all, and thus the *Amidah* concludes with this prayer for peace:

> Grant peace, welfare, blessing, grace, kindness, and mercy to us and unto all Israel, Your people. Bless us, O our Father, even all of us together, with the light of Your countenance. For by the light of Your countenance You have given us, O Lord our God, the Torah of life, lovingkindness and righteousness, blessing, mercy, life, and peace. May it be good in Your sight to bless Your people Israel at all times and in every hour with your peace. Praised are You, O Lord, who blesses your people Israel with peace.

THE *AMIDAH* FOR THE SABBATH AND FESTIVALS

The *Amidah* prayer for the Sabbath and festivals consists only of seven blessings. The first three and the last three blessings are the same as those said in the daily *Amidah*, but the middle section differs. Instead of petitions that ask God for a variety of needs, the single blessing for the Sabbath and festivals emphasizes the holiness of the day. This is because the *Jerusalem Talmud* (*Shabbat 15:3*) states that petitioning God for personal needs is strictly forbidden.

Thus the middle paragraph and blessing of the Sabbath and festival *Amidah* consists of a paragraph called *kedushat hayom* (the sanctification of the day). It is the same in every service:

> Our God and God of our ancestors accept our rest. Sanctify us through Your commandments, And set our portion in Your *Torah*. Gratify us with Your goodness, and make us happy through Your salvation. Purify our hearts to serve You in truth. Give us Your holy Sabbath, Lord our God, with love and favor as our heritage. May Israel who sanctifies Your name rest thereon. Praised are You, God, who sanctifies the Sabbath.

The middle blessing of the *Amidah* for festivals again praises God for hallowing the festivals. It also petitions God that we may serve God in truth and that our hearts be purified. These petitions relate to the spiritual needs of the worshipper.

> Lord our God bestow upon us the blessing of Your Festivals, for life and for peace, for joy and for gladness, even as You have promised. Our God and God of our ancestors, add holiness to our lives with Your mitzvot and let Your Torah be our portion. Fill our lives with goodness and make us happy with Your triumph. Purify our hearts so that we may serve You faithfully. O Lord our God grant that we inherit Your holy gift of Festivals so that the people Israel who hallow Your name will rejoice in You. Praised are You, God, who hallows the people Israel and the Festivals.

Grace After Meals:
Birkat Hamazon

The *Birkat Hamazon,* popularly known as *benshen* (from the Latin *benedicere*), is the grace recited after meals that included bread. It is based on the biblical command: 'When you eat and are satisfied, you shall bless the Lord your God for the good land He has given you.' (*Deuteronomy 8:10*) It consists of four blessings, three of which are of high antiquity; the fourth, of later origin, was instituted after Bar Kochba's defeat about 135 of the Common Era.

According to a Talmudic statement, the first paragraph was composed by Moses, the second by Joshua, the third by David and Solomon, and the fourth by the sages (*Talmud Berachot 48a*). The first is an acknowledgment of God as the sustainer of all creatures. The second is a thanksgiving for the grant of the Torah and the Land of Israel. The third blessing is a petition for the restoration of Zion and Jerusalem. The fourth blessing is an expression of thanksgiving for the general benefits and favors bestowed upon many by his Creator.

Rabbi Abraham Kook regards the original three blessings as a series of spiritually ascending levels. A person's first concern is and must be with his physical survival. Once physical survival is assured, one can turn one's attention to the attainment of spiritual aspirations, such as the hope that Jerusalem will be the spiritual center of the Jewish people.

Following is a synopsis of the four blessings of the Grace After meals.

FIRST BLESSING: *BIRKAT HAZAN*
(BLESSING FOR FOOD)

The first blessing reads as follows:

> Praised are You, Lord our God, Sovereign of the Universe, who in
> His goodness, grace, kindness, and mercy, feeds the whole world.
> God gives food to all flesh, for God's loving kindness is eternal.
> In God's great goodness, we have never lacked for food. May we
> never lack for food, for the sake of God's great name. For God
> nourishes and sustains everything, does good to all, and prepares
> food for all God's creatures that He created. Praised are You, God,
> who provides food for all.

This blessing provides the basic theme for the entire Grace after
the meal. It proclaims God as the One who nourishes all things
and expresses gratitude for God's ability to sustain the entire world.
Obviously, one ethical implication of someone who is grateful for his
or her food involves taking care of the earth, so that others can be fed
as well. To thank God for a gift and not take responsibility for it, to
abuse food or to deny the rights of those it took to bring us that food,
is to deny God and the gift that God has given us.

SECOND BLESSING: *BIRKAT HAARETZ*
(BLESSING FOR THE LAND)

This blessing reads as follows:

> We thank You, Lord our God, because you did give us as a heritage
> to our ancestors a desirable, good and ample land, and because
> you did bring us forth, O Lord our God, from the land of Egypt,
> and did deliver us from the house of bondage. As well as for your
> covenant which you have sealed in our flesh, your Torah which You
> have taught us, Your statutes which You have made known to us,
> the life, grace and loving kindness which You have bestowed upon
> us, and for the food wherewith you constantly feed and sustain us
> every day, in every season, and in every hour. For everything, Lord

our God, we thank You and bless You. May Your name be blessed in the mouth of all living continually and forever, as it is written, 'And you shall eat and be satisfied, and bless the Lord your God for the good land which God has given you.' Praised are You, O God, for the land and for the food.

After the first blessing, the oldest universal blessing, comes the second blessing, the national one. In it, we thank God for the Land of Israel and the redemption from Egyptian bondage. Israel is the second home to the Jewish people, and is an important player in the spiritual development of the Jewish people. Thus when reciting the Grace after the meal the Jew is constantly reminded of the importance of the Land of Israel to the sustenance and very survival of the Jewish people.

One pundit has pointed out that if we change the letter *chaf* in the Hebrew word *uverachta* (and bless) to *chet*, we change the meaning of the biblical verse (*Deuteronomy 8:7*) quoted in the second blessing 'for the Lord your God brings you into a good land...and you shall eat and be satisfied, and *run away*' (without saying grace). It is an old story: how often do we fail to express any appreciation for the blessings of life. The Grace after the meal provides us with a wonderful opportunity each meal to express such gratitude for life's bounty.

THIRD BLESSING: *BIRKAT YERUSHALAYIM* (BLESSING FOR JERUSALEM)

This blessing reads as follows:

Be compassionate, O Lord our God, to Your people Israel, to Your city, Jerusalem, and to Zion, the dwelling place of Your glory, to the royal House of David, Your anointed, and to the great and holy Temple that was called by Your name. Our God, our Father, tend us, feed us, sustain us, maintain us, and comfort us. Grant us quick relief, Lord our God, from all of our troubles. Lord our God let us not be in need of other people's gifts or loans, but only Your filled and open hand, holy and bountiful. So that we may never be ashamed or humiliated. Rebuild Jerusalem, the holy city, soon in our days. Praised are You, God, who in His mercy builds Jerusalem. Amen.

Originally the third blessing of *Birkat Hamazon* was a blessing of gratitude for Jerusalem and the Temple. After the Temple was destroyed and Jerusalem torn asunder was the blessing reworded as a prayer for their rebuilding and rejuvenation.

According to the *Talmud* (*Berachot 49a*), 'one who does not mention the kingdom of the House of David' (*i.e.*, Jerusalem) has not fulfilled his obligation. Indeed Jerusalem is the most important city of the Bible and has been the focal point of Jewish religious life and aspirations ever since David made it the City of David.

Only this, the third blessing, ends with *Amen*, for originally it was the last one and the Grace after meals ended her.

FOURTH BLESSING: *BIRKAT HATOV V'HAMETIV* (BLESSING OF GOODNESS)

Following are the words of the fourth blessing of the Grace after the meal:

> Praised are You, Lord our God, Ruler of the Universe, God of our Father and Sovereign. Our Mighty One, our Creator, our Redeemer, our Fashioner; our Holy One, the Holy One of Jacob; our Shepherd, the Shepherd of Israel. You are the Sovereign the King who is good and does good to all. For every day God has done good to us, does good to us and will do good to us. It is God who has bestowed, does bestow and will always bestow upon us grace, kindness, mercy and relief; rescue, success, blessing, salvation, consolation, sustenance, and maintenance; mercy, life, peace and all good; and of everything good may we never lack.

According to Maimonides, the fourth blessing to the Grace after meals was prescribed by the rabbis of the *Mishnah* soon after the destruction of the second Temple in Jerusalem. (Maimonides, commentary to *Mishnah, Berachot 6:8*). This blessing was added in tragic circumstances. In the year 137 CE after the failure of the revolt of Bar Kochba against the Romans who had ruled Israel with such brutality, and after all the Jews in the last stronghold at Bethar had been slain, the Roman Emperor Hadrian refused the Jews permission to bury their dead. Though their army had been decimated and their dead lay unburied, the rabbis of that time nevertheless added to the grace after every meal a fourth blessing related to God's great goodness. Thus did the Jews refuse to lose faith in God's abiding goodness, and the blessing offers the one who recites the blessing constant courage and a reminder to never lose hope because God's mercy will always redeem the Israelites.

These four blessings constitute the 'statutory' Grace after the meals according to the *Talmud*. But, like the prayer book itself, the Grace continued to grow become some Jews felt that the four blessings did not fully express all of their needs and hopes. Therefore, from time to time, they added to the four blessings. Among the additions was a group of requests couched in a formula that began *Harachaman* – may the Merciful One. The texts of these vary, but all versions contain a prayer for the host and for those present, a prayer for the coming of Elijah the prophet, and a prayer that we may be worthy to see the days of the Messiah.

The Grace after the meals ends with a prayer for peace. With the expression of thanks for food we thus also pray each time for peace, which will make it possible for us to always enjoy these blessings.

By saying the *Birkat Hamazon* at the conclusion of every meal, one has an opportunity to endow the routine act of eat with lasting significance. It is a constant reminder never to take the act of eating for granted and our ethical responsibility to become a partner with God so that all humanity will be sustained.

LAWS CONCERNING SAYING GRACE AFTER MEALS

Following are several laws related to the recitation of the blessings of the Grace after the meal, as culled from the condensed version of the *Code of Jewish Law*:

- The tablecloth and the bread must still remain on the table when Grace is recited, to indicate the abundance of food which the Lord, blessed be His name, has supplied for us, in that He gives enough to eat and to spare.

- It is customary to either remove the knives left on the table before reciting Grace, or else to cover them. For the table is compared to an altar, and concerning the altar, it is written (*Deuteronomy 27:5*): 'You shall not lift up any iron upon them.' For iron shortens the life of a man while the altar prolongs life, and it is improper that one which shortens life should be raised on one that prolongs it. The table also prolongs the days of man and atones for his sins if one invites poor wayfarers at his table. The power of hospitality is so great that it causes the Divine Presence to be in our midst. The custom prevails in many communities not to cover the knives on the Sabbath or on festivals. For on weekdays they represent the brutal might of Esau, but on the Sabbath and festivals there is no Satan or evil occurrence.

- Even if we have eaten only a piece of bread no larger than the size of an olive, we must say the Grace thereafter.

- Grace after meals should be recited neither standing nor walking, but sitting. If we have walked to and fro in the house while eating, or if we have been standing or reclining, we must sit when reciting the Grace, in order that we may recite it with devotion. While saying Grace, we should not recline our seats, because it is indicative of pride, but we should sit erect, put on the coat and hat, in order that the fear of Heaven be upon us, and that our minds be concentrated upon saying the Grace with reverence and awe. We are not allowed to do anything else while reciting Grace.

- If we neglect to recite Grace up to the time the food has become digested, that is, when we begin to feel hungry, we can no longer make amends and say Grace. Some are of the opinion that food is digested in one and one fifth hours. Nevertheless, at big feasts, people occasionally tarry longer than this time limit between the eating and the saying of Grace, for the reason that also in the interim they drink and eat desserts. However, it is best not to wait too long.

- If we violate the law and leave the table before reciting Grace, then if at the place where we are now there is a piece of bread, we should partake thereof without saying the blessing *hamotzi*, and thereafter say Grace.
- If we are in doubt as to whether or not we have recited Grace, then if we are still satiated, we must recite Grace again (for the saying of Grace is then a Mosaic ordinance). If we happen to fall asleep in the middle of reciting Grace, and upon awakening we do not know where we left off, we must repeat from the beginning.
- If a non-Jew is present in the room when Grace is recited, we should add: Us, the sons of the covenant, all of us together.'

Torah and *Haftarah* Blessings

The two benedictions pronounced over the *Torah* by the person honored with an *aliyah* contain forty words, which are said to allude to the forty days spent by Moses on Mount Sinai. These blessings, each of which consists of an identical number of words (twenty), are quoted in the *Talmudic* tractate of *Berachot 11b*).

Originally, the first Torah blessing was said by the first person before he began to read, and the second blessing was said only by the last person after he had completed his reading. Those in between read their portion without reciting any blessings at all.

During the period of the *Talmud*, the rabbis ruled that every person who came up to the *Torah* scroll had to recite both blessings. According to the Talmudic tractate of *Megillah* (*21b*), this innovation was introduced so as not to deprive any congregational member (*i.e.,* those arriving after the commencement of the *Torah* reading or those leaving before the end) the opportunity to hear both *Torah* blessings.

As time passed, the number of people with the capability of reading from the *Torah* decreased. In order to reduce the embarrassment of those who could not read from the *Torah*, a new custom arose of a *Torah* reader who would read on behalf of the one called to the *Torah*.

Here are the two Torah blessings:

1. Praised are You, Lord our God, Ruler of the universe, who chose us from among all peoples by giving us God's *Torah*. Praised are You, God, who gives the *Torah*.

2. Praised are You, Lord our God, Ruler of the universe, who gave
   us a *Torah* of truth and planted within us lasting life. Praised are
   You, God, who gives the *Torah*.

FIRST *TORAH* BLESSING

The first *Torah* blessing praises God for giving the Israelites the *Torah*
and for having chosen the Israelites as God's special people. Having
rejected the traditional understanding of the chosen-ness concept,
Reform and Reconstructionist prayer books have modified this blessing to state that 'God brought us near to His service.'

SECOND *TORAH* BLESSING

This blessing expresses gratitude to God for giving the Israelites a
Torah of truth and planted within them eternal life. Some commentators have asserted that the use of the phrase 'planted within us eternal
life' is a reference to the Oral *Torah*, paralleling *Ecclesiastes 12:11*: 'The
words of the sages are planted...'

THE *HAFTARAH* BLESSINGS

The word *Haftarah* means conclusion, and today refers to the prophetic section recited after the reading of the *Torah* on Sabbaths and
festivals. Usually, though not always, the *Haftarah* contains some
reference to an incident mentioned in the assigned *Torah* reading.

   In his commentary on liturgy, Rabbi David Abudarham of four-
teenth-century Spain traces the custom of reading from the Prophets
after the *Torah* reading back to the period of persecution preceding the
Maccabean revolt. According to him, the *Haftarah* was instituted as a
substitute for the *Torah* reading, prohibited under the severe decree
of Antiochus Ephiphanes.

   Some authorities have suggested that the readings from the Prophets may have been instituted to emphasize the great value of these
books to the *Torah* of Moses. This was done in order to oppose the

Samaritans who refused to recognize the sanctity of the Prophets. This sect, which originated in the early years of the Second Temple in the district of Samaria, Palestine, strictly observed the precepts of the *Pentateuch*, but rejected not only the rabbinic interpretation and tradition but also the prophetic writings.

The *Haftarah* is bracketed by blessings before and after it. There is one single blessing preceding it, and five following it. Some have said that the five *Haftarah* blessings symbolize the five books of Moses, whose teachings the Prophets came to implement.

Following are the five Haftarah blessings and a brief synopsis of the themes of each one.

FIRST *HAFTARAH* BLESSING:

This single blessing before the *Haftarah* praises God for the faithful and truthful words of the messengers of God.

> Praised are You, O Lord our God, Ruler of the universe, who has chosen good prophets and has been pleased with their faithful words. Praised are You, O Lord, who has singled out the *Torah*, Moses as Your servant, Israel as Your people, and prophets of truth and righteousness.

Since there were a variety of false prophets who arose throughout the course of Jewish history, the blessing emphasizes the fact that God's prophets prophesied accurately and truthfully. The blessing also thanks God for the *Torah* and for those who have passed the *Torah* from generation to generation.

SECOND *HAFTARAH* BLESSING

This blessing, the first one chanted after the *Haftarah*, voices praise for the truthfulness and fulfillment of God's words. It is also a blessing and a prayer for the fulfillment of God's prophecies, which are truthful and reliable.

Praised are You, Lord our God, Ruler of the universe, Creator of all worlds, righteous in all generations, the faithful God who says and does, who speaks and fulfills for all of the Lord's words are truthful and just. You are faithful, Lord our God, and all of Your words are to be trusted. Not one of Your words is empty, for You are a faithful and merciful God. Be praised, O Lord, God whose words can be trusted.

THIRD *HAFTARAH* BLESSING

The third Haftarah blessing asks for mercy upon Zion and the entire household of Israel.

Have mercy upon Zion, for it is the source of our life. Save the oppressed of soul speedily in our days. Be praised, O God, who makes Zion rejoice in her children.

FOURTH *HAFTARAH* BLESSING

This blessing parallels the fifteenth blessing of the *Amidah*. It voices the hope for the coming of Elijah and the messianic kingdom. The restoration of the House of David is a byproduct of Messianic redemption.

Make us happy, O Lord our God, with the coming of Your servant, Elijah the Prophet, and with the establishment of the kingdom of the house of David, Your messiah. May he come soon and bring joy to our hearts. May no stranger sit on his throne, nor others assume for themselves his glory. For You have promised by Your holy name that his light will never go out. Be praised O God, the Shield of David.

FIFTH *HAFTARAH* BLESSING

The fifth and final blessing is an overall blessing of gratitude for the *Torah*, for the privilege of worshiping God, for the prophets and for the Sabbath that was given to the Children of Israel.

For the Torah, for worship, for the prophets, and for this Sabbath day which You have given to us, O Lord our God, for holiness and rest, for honor and for glory, for all of these, O Lord our God, we thank You and praise You. May Your name be praised continually in the mouth of all that lives. Praised are You O God, who sanctifies the Sabbath.

Priestly Blessing

The priestly blessing, expressed in three biblical verses and chanted at the end of every *Amidah* prayer, was part of the daily service in ancient times in the Temple. Every morning and evening the priests raised their hands aloft and pronounced the *birkat kohanim* (priestly blessing) from a special platform, called *a duchan*.

The priestly blessing is pronounced only at a public synagogue service with the required quorum of ten adults. In Israel, the custom is to recite it every Sabbath both at the *Shacharit* morning and *Musaf* (additional) service in Jerusalem. Ashkenazi custom in traditional settings is to recite it only on the High Holy Days and three pilgrim festivals (Sukkot, Passover, and Shavuot). Sephardic custom is for the *kohanim* to bless the worshippers every day. In Conservative Judaism the recital of the priestly blessing is optional. It sometimes is recited in Reform, Conservative and Reconstructionist settings by the rabbi as a closing blessing at the end of the service. Bar and Bat Mitzvah children may also be blessed by their rabbis with the invoking of the priestly blessing.

In order for the *kohanim* to properly recite the blessing in the synagogue, those of priestly descent remove their shoes, wash their hands, and ascend the *bimah* in front of the ark. They then face the congregation, and with fingers stretched in a symbolic arrangement underneath the *tallit* (prayer shawl) covering their face, they repeat the priestly blessing word for word after the Prayer Leader. Their hands are held touching at the thumbs with the first two fingers of each separated from the other two, thus forming a sort of fan. This figure became the device of the kohanim and is often inscribed on their tombstones. In rabbinic literature, the priestly blessing also came to be known as *nesiat kapayim* (raising of the hands).

The custom is not to look at the *kohanim* while they are reciting the priestly blessing. In many communities the father draws his children to himself and covers them with his prayer shawl. The reason for this behavior is that the *Talmud* (*Hagigah 16a*) states that those who look at the *kohanim* while they are reciting the Priestly blessing will 'have their eyes dimmed' (i.e., the radiance of God's Presence will be too much for the people to bear).

There is a widespread custom to respond *Amen* after each of the three sections of the priestly blessing, when said by the *kohanim*, but 'so may it be Your will' when the Cantor or Prayer Leader recites it.

Here are the words of the Priestly Blessing, whose biblical origins is *Numbers 6:24–26*:

May the Lord bless you and protect you.
May the Lord let His countenance shine upon you and be gracious to you.
May the Lord look kindly on you and grant you peace.

The blessing has been interpreted in many ways. Some commentators assert that the first part of the blessing is for material goods, the second part of the blessing for intellectual endeavors, and the last part of the blessing for mental and spiritual wellbeing. The *Targum*, the ancient Aramaic translation of the Torah, provides an authoritative insight into the meaning of these three blessings. The first is intended to be a blessing for success in one's work and for protection in precarious situations. The second blessing is a request for enlightenment through the study of *Torah*. The third blessing is a plea that God will listen to the worshippers when they turn to Him in prayer. It concludes with a prayer for peace in every area of life.

Interestingly, the *Birkat Kohanim* is the only *mitzvah* whose accompanying blessing stipulates that it must be performed with love. (*b'ahavah*) The implication here is that for one to bestow God's blessing on another, one must be filled with love for his fellow Jew.

LAWS OF THE PRIESTLY BLESSING

Following is a synopsis of the laws related to the *Birkat Kohanim* as culled from the condensed version of the *Code of Jewish Law*.

1. According to the Law of Moses (*Numbers 6:22–27*), *kohanim* must bless the people, for it is written: 'Thus shall you bless the people.' If a *kohen* who is not disqualified, refuses to go up to bless the people, he is guilty of transgressing a Divine Command. However, he is not considered a violator of the law, unless he is called upon to do so.

   It is customary in our regions for the *kohanim* to bless the people only on festivals, because the people rejoice in the holiday, and on *Yom Kippur* because there is rejoicing on account of their having obtained forgiveness and pardon of sins, for only the merry of heart should bless, which is not true of other days. Even on Sabbaths they are worried about their livelihood and their being restrained from work. And on a festival they only bless the people at the *musaf* (additional) service because they will soon leave the synagogue and rejoice with the festival.

2. The *kohanim* should neither drink wine nor any other intoxicating beverage before their blessing. If a *kohen* feels faint and he desires to eat some pastry before the *musaf*, he should listen to someone else's *kiddush*.

3. Before pronouncing the blessing, the *kohanim* must wash their hands up to the wrist, just as the *kohanim* did before their service in the Temple, as it is written (*Psalms 134:2*): 'Lift up your hands in holiness, and bless the Lord.' It is doubtful whether a blessing should be pronounced over this ablution, since such a blessing has already been uttered upon rising in the morning. Because of the doubt, the custom prevails not to pronounce the blessing.

4. A Levite pours the water upon the hands of the *kohanim*, as it is written (*Numbers 18:6*): 'And your brethren also, the tribe of Levi…bring you near with you, that they may be joined to you, and minister unto you.' If no Levite is present, a firstborn of the mother pours the water, and if there is no firstborn present, it is better that the *kohen* himself should pour the water on his hands,

rather than an Israelite. If the hands of the Levite or of the firstborn who is to pour the water upon the hands of the *kohen* are unclean, he must first wash them.

5. The *kohanim* are forbidden to go up to the platform with their shoes on. They should remove them before washing their hands. Out of respect for the public, they should hide their shoes under the benches where they cannot be seen.

6. After they mount the platform, they remain standing, facing the Holy Ark in the east, and after saying *Modim* (we give thanks) with the congregation, they say: 'May it be Your will, O Lord our God, that this blessing wherewith You have commanded us to bless Your people Israel, be perfect without any flaw or error from now and forever…' After the *hazan* has called *Kohanim*, they begin the blessing, all saying in unison: 'Blessed are You, O Lord our God, King of the universe, who has sanctified us by the holiness of Aaron'; then turning their faces toward the people, they conclude: 'And God commanded us in love to bless His people Israel,' to which the congregation responds *Amen*. The *hazan* should not respond *Amen*, as this would constitute an interruption in his prayer.

7. They (the *kohanim*) raise their hands to the level of their shoulders, and separate their fingers in such a way that there are five spaces between them; between the two fingers on each side there is one space, and between the fingers and the thumb there is another space, the same with the other hand, making it a total of four spaces, and between the thumbs of the two hands there is another space. In all there are five spaces. This must be done, because it is written (*Song of Songs 2:9*): 'He peers through the lattice' (*hecharakim*, five openings). The right hand should be raised slightly above the left, the right thumb being above the left thumb. They should, however, spread their hands in such a way that the palms be turned toward the ground and the back of their hands toward heaven.

8. When the *kohanim* bless the people, they should neither look around nor divert their thoughts, but their eyes should be directed downward as in prayer. The people should pay attention to the

blessing and face the *kohanim*, but they should not gaze at them, nor should the *kohanim* gaze at their hands. It is for this reason that the *kohanim* pull the *tallit* over their faces, extending their hands outside. The worshipers also cover their faces with the *tallit* in order not to gaze at the *kohanim*.

9. The *hazan* recites the priestly blessing word for word, and the *kohanim* repeat after him. The congregation responds *Amen* at the conclusion of the first, second and third verses. The *hazan* should not recite the priestly blessing from memory but from a prayer book, so that he may not get confused. He may also respond *Amen* after the verses, which is not considered an interruption, because it is part of the prayer.

10. When the *kohanim* repeat the words of the blessings, the congregation should not recite any verse, but should listen attentively to each word pronounced by the *kohanim*.

11. An effort should be made not to have a *kohen* act as *hazan*. And if the *hazan* happens to be a *kohen*, he should not go up to bless the people, neither should he prompt the *kohanim*, but someone else should stand by him to call *kohanim*, and all to read the words of the blessing.

12. If a congregation consists of *kohanim* only, then if they are no more than ten, all go up to say the blessing. Whom do they bless? Their brethren in the countryside. And who responds *Amen*? The women and the little children. If no women and children are present, the lack of the *Amen* response does not hinder the priestly blessing.

13. If a *kohen* who had already blessed the congregation visits another synagogue, he may go up to pronounce the blessing again. But if he is not inclined, he is not obliged to go up even if he hears the call *Kohanim*, inasmuch as he has already done his duty.

14. A *kohen* who has a blemish on his face, may go up to pronounce the priestly blessing, since it is the custom in our communities that the *kohanim* pull the *tallit* over their faces. However, a *kohen* who has a defect in his hands, like a white scurf or spots, or they are crooked, or he is unable to part his fingers, he is not allowed to bless the people, because the worshipers will look at his hands

and be distracted. A *kohen* who is unable to pronounce the letters properly, interchanging the *shin* and the *sin*, should not go up to say the priestly blessing unless the entire congregation read thus.

Blessings of the Moon and Sun

BLESSING OF THE MOON

The blessing of the new moon is recited in the open air when the moon is visible between the fourth and the sixteenth of the month, preferably on a Saturday night, after *Havdalah*, when the observant Jew is in a joyous frame of mind. This festive ceremony of ancient origin is fully discussed in the *Talmud* (*Sanhedrin 42a; Sofrim 20:1–2*). The moon, appearing periodically in several phases, has been looked upon as symbolic of the Jewish people whose history consists of varied phrases. Also, like the moon, the Jews regularly reappear after being temporarily eclipsed.

The four synonyms referring to the Creator in one of the passages of the blessing over the moon have as their initials the letters which spell the name *Yaakov* – Jacob, alluding to his descendants, the people of Israel.

The expression 'long live David, King of Israel' refers to *Psalm 89:38*, which says that David's dynasty shall 'like the moon be established forever'. The numerical value of the Hebrew words *David melech Yisrael chai ve'kaym* (819) is equal to that of *rosh chodesh* (new moon). It was the password of Bar Kochba's army. Following is the text for the blessing of the new moon:

> Rabbi Yochanan said: Whoever blesses the new moon at the proper time is considered as having welcomed the presence of the *Shechhina. Halleluyah.* Praised God from the heavens. Praise God, angels on high. Praise God, sun and moon and all shining stars. Praise God, highest heavens. Let them praise the glory of God at whose command they were created, at whose command

they endure forever and by whose laws nature abides (*Psalm 148:1–6*).

Praised are You, Lord our God, Ruler of the universe, whose words created the heavens, whose breath created all that they contain. Statutes and seasons God set for them, that they should not deviate from their assigned task. Happily, gladly, they do the will of their Creator, whose work is dependable. To the moon God spoke: Renew yourself, crown of glory for those who were born in the womb, who also are destined to be renewed and to extol their Creator for His glorious sovereignty. Praised are You, God, who renews the months. David, King of Israel, lives and endures.

In the Talmudic tractate of *Sofrim* (*20:1–2*), several mystifying details are prescribed in connection with the new moon blessing. They are as follows:

> The blessing of the moon must take place at the conclusion of the Sabbath, when one is in a jolly mood and dressed in nice garments. The worshiper should look steadily at the moon, join straight his feet, and recite the blessing…He should say three times *siman tov* (a good sign) and perform three dancing gestures in the direction of the moon while saying three times: Just as I cannot touch you, may my enemies never be able to harm me…Then he should say *shalom* (peace) to his neighbor three times and go home with a happy heart.

BLESSING OF THE SUN

The rabbis taught that a person who sees the sun at its turning point, the moon in its power, the planets in their orbits, or the signs of the zodiac in their order should recite, 'Blessed are You who makes the work of creation.' This opportunity occurs every twenty-eight years or when the signs of the zodiac in their orderly progress begin again (*Talmud Berachot 59b*).

The blessing of the sun, *birkat hachamah* is a prayer service in which the sun is blessed in thanksgiving for its being created and set into motion in the firmament on the fourth day of creation. The ceremony itself takes place once every twenty-eight years, after the *Shacharit* morning service, when the sun is about ninety degrees above the eastern horizon, on the first Wednesday of the month of *Nisan*.

First, participants recite *Psalms 84:12, 75:5* and *75:2, Malachi 3:20, Psalms 97:6* and *Psalm 148*. This is followed by the blessing: *Baruch Ata Adonai Eloheinu melech ha'olam oseh ma'asey v'resheet* (Praised are You, Lord our God, source of Creation'). Next, *Psalms 19* and *121* are read, followed by the hymn *El Adon*. The ritual ends with a thanksgiving prayer in which the community expresses gratitude to God for sustaining it.

Since the blessing of the sun is recited on the day on which the sun returns to its very spot in the heavens which it occupied at the moment of its original creation, it creates awareness on the part of the worshiper of the process of creation itself and its wondrous nature. God is acknowledged as the eternal conservator of the universe and the blessing can arouse a person from his or her lethargy and force one to reflect upon this magnificent cosmic phenomenon.

(NOTE: The Jewish community last blessed the sun on April 8, 1953 March 18, 1981 and April 7, 2009. The next time that the sun is scheduled to be blessed is on April 8, 2037.)

LAWS OF *BIRKAT HACHAMAH*

Following is a brief summary of some of the important laws and customs related to the blessing of the sun.

1. A quorum of ten adults is not required for the recitation of the blessing of the sun. It is preferable, however, to recite the blessing in the company of a large assemblage of people.
2. Some authorities maintain that it is preferable to pronounce the blessing immediately upon seeing the sun in the morning. Others maintain that it is preferable to pronounce the blessing outside the synagogue after morning services. If clouds threaten to obscure the sun, all agree that the blessing should be recited without delay.

3. The blessing should be recited while standing.
4. The blessing may be recited while standing under a roof or even when observing the sun through a window from inside a building.
5. The blessing should not be recited if the sun is obscured by clouds. However, the blessing may be recited on a cloudy day if the outline of the sun can be perceived beneath the clouds or if any portion of the sun is visible between the clouds.
6. The *shehecheyanu* blessing is not recited in conjunction with the blessing of the sun.
7. Minors who have reached the age of training in mitzvot and who understand the nature of a blessing should be taught to recite the blessing.
8. The blessing of the sun is recited on *Yom Tov* even when the occasion for its recitation coincides with the festival of Passover.

Birchot Hanehenin: Blessings of Enjoyment

According to Maimonides, the medieval Jewish philosopher, there are three types of blessings:

1. Blessings recited prior to the performance of a *mitzvah*, known as *birchot hamitzvot*.
2. Blessings that express praise of God and thanks to God, as well as those that ask God for things, called *birchot hodaah*.
3. Blessings recited prior to eating, drinking, or smelling nice things, called *birchot hanehenin*.

This chapter presents the variety of blessings recited prior to eating, drinking, or smelling sweet fragrances.

FOOD BLESSINGS

Reciting blessings before partaking of food is the Jewish way of sanctifying the routine act of eating. The *Talmud* says that the table upon which we eat is like the altar of the Temple. The whole process of eating is thus changed into a beautiful ceremony. Jews are bidden to wash their hands before breaking bread, not simply to cleanse them, but because the priests washed their hands before they offered sacrifices. The *hamotzi*, the blessing of the bread begins the meal, reminding the participants from whose goodness and kindness the food comes. Thus, Judaism is able to take something which is common and ordinary, namely the act of eating, and raise it to an act of holiness.

BLESSING OVER BREAD

Praised are You, Lord our God, Ruler of the universe who brings forth bread from the earth.

BLESSING OVER FOOD (OTHER THAN BREAD) PREPARED FROM WHEAT, BARLEY, RYE, OATS OR SPELT

Praised are You, Lord our God, Ruler of the universe who creates various kinds of nourishment.

BLESSING OVER WINE OR GRAPE JUICE

Praised are You, Lord our God, Ruler of the universe who creates fruit of the vine.

BLESSING OVER FRUIT

Praised are You, Lord our God, Ruler of the universe, who creates fruit of the tree.

BLESSING FOR FOOD WHICH GROWS IN THE GROUND

Praised are You, Lord our God, Ruler of the universe, who creates fruit of the ground.

BLESSING FOR OTHER FOOD OR DRINK

Praised are You, Lord our God, Ruler of the universe, at whose word all things come into being.

LAWS OF BLESSINGS BEFORE
ENJOYING FOOD AND DRINK

Following is a synopsis of the important general laws related to blessings over food.

1. It is written (*Psalm 24:1*): 'The earth is the Lord's and the fullness thereof,' which implies that everything is like consecrated matter. Thus it is forbidden to derive any pleasure from this world without first thanking the Almighty by pronouncing a blessing. One who enjoys things without uttering a blessing is like one who had committed a trespass against the Sanctuary of God, blessed be the One. There is no set quantity of food or drink over which a blessing must be uttered. No matter how little we eat or drink, we must first pronounce the appropriate blessing.

2. It is our duty to learn the various blessings and say the one that is appropriate to the kind of food.

3. We should take the article over which we are about to utter the blessing in the right hand before eating, drinking, scenting, or performing a precept thereby, and ascertain which blessing we must say, so that when we mention the Divine Name, which is the most important part of the blessing, we may know how to conclude it. If we say the blessing over the article without taking it in our hand, but so long as it has been before us at that time, our duty is done. However, if the article is not before us when reciting the blessing, but has been brought later, even if we had it in mind while saying the blessing, the blessing must be repeated.

4. If we have taken some fruit to eat and after uttering the blessing it fell out of our hand and was lost, or it became too loathsome to be eaten; or if we have said the benediction over a glass of liquor and spilt it, if at that time there was no more of the same kind of food or liquor before us, and it was our intention to consume more than that which was in our hand, the blessing which we said referred also to whatever remained before us, and we need not repeat the blessing.

5. The pause between the saying of the blessing and the consumption of the food should not be longer than it takes to say *Shalom alecha, Rabbi u'mori* (Peace be unto you, my Master and teacher).

6. If we taste food to ascertain if it needs any salt, or for any other similar purpose, and we reject it, we need not say a blessing over it. However, if we swallow it, it is doubtful whether or not we need say a blessing.

7. If we drink some beverage or eat some bread or any other kind of food, for the purpose of dislodging something that has stuck in the throat, we must utter its preceding and concluding blessings.

THE BLESSINGS *BORAY PERI HA'ETZ, BORAY PERI HA'ADAMAH,* AND *SHEHAKOL*

1. One says the blessing *boray peri ha'etz* (who created the fruit of the tree) over fruit that grows on trees. On partaking of the produce

which grow in or close to the ground, such as turnips, vegetables, beans, and herbs, one says the blessing *boray peri ha'adamah* (who created the fruit of the ground). A tree, to be designated by this name, must have branches that do not perish in the winter, and which produce leaves in the spring, even though the leaves be as thin as the stalks of flax. But a plant whose branches perish in the winter although its root remains, is not called a 'tree', and over its fruit we say the blessing *boray peri ha'adamah*.

2. Before partaking of food which is not the produce of the soil, such as meat, fish, milk, and cheese, and before drinking any beverage other than wine and olive oil, we say the benediction *shehakol* (that all is according to God's will).

3. Although mushrooms and truffles receive their nutrition from the moisture of the earth, since their growth depends, not upon the soil but upon the atmosphere, they cannot be called 'fruit of the ground.' Therefore, the blessing *shehakol* should be pronounced over them.

4. The blessings *boray peri ha'etz* and *boray peri ha'adamah* should be said only after articles of food which can be eaten raw, and it is customary to eat in this state. But if it is customary to eat them only when cooked, although it is also fit to eat them raw, nevertheless when eaten raw, the blessing *shehakol* should be said over it. Pickled food is considered the same as cooked food.

5. Before eating radishes, one should say the blessing *boray peri ha'adamah*. Likewise, the blessing *boray peri ha'adamah* is said over garlic and onions that are soft and can be eaten raw, although they are generally eaten with bread.

6. If one eats cooked articles of food that taste better when raw, one says the blessing *shehakol*.

7. Herbs which grow spontaneously without cultivation and are fit to eat raw, although one has cooked them so that they are a proper dish, are not considered fruit of the ground, and the blessing *shehakol* should be said over them. However, one should say the blessing *boray peri ha'adamah* over lettuce and similar vegetables that have been planted.

8. We say the blessing *boray peri ha'adamah* over the seeds of fruit if they are sweet. If they are bitter, they require no blessing. But the blessing *shehakol* is said over them if we make them palatable by roasting over fire or in any other way.

9. There are certain types of fruit which contain juice in their kernels, and while the kernels are not fit to eat, the juice extracted from them is palatable. The blessing *shehakol* should be said over such juice.

10. We neither say the blessing *boray peri ha'etz* nor *boray peri ha'adamah* unless we can at least slightly recognize the fruit. But if they are so crushed that they are unrecognizable, as in the case with plum jam, or crushed peas, the blessing to be said over them is *shehakol*.

11. We say the blessing *shehakol* over sugar. Also, we say the blessing *shehakol* when one chews sugar cane or cinnamon or licorice, and only the taste of it is enjoyed, while the bulk is thrown away.

BLESSINGS OVER FRAGRANCES

There are several blessings related to our sense of smell, and appreciation for the ability to sense a sweet fragrance. Following are the traditional blessings that one recites for the blessings of smell.

BLESSING UPON SMELLING FRAGRANT SPICES
Praised are You, Lord our God, Ruler of the universe, who creates various spices.

BLESSING UPON SMELLING FRAGRANCE OF TREES OR SHRUBS
Praised are You, Lord our God, Ruler of the universe, who creates fragrant trees.

BLESSING UPON SMELLING FRAGRANCE OF HERBS OR PLANTS
Praised are You, Lord our God, Ruler of the universe, who creates fragrant plants.

BLESSING UPON SMELLING FRAGRANT FRUIT
Praised are You, Lord our God, Ruler of the universe, who gives a pleasant fragrance to fruits.

BLESSING UPON SMELLING FRAGRANT OIL
Praised are You, Lord our God, Ruler of the universe who creates fragrant oil.

LAWS RELATED TO BLESSINGS OVER FRAGRANCES

Here are several laws related to fragrance blessings, as cited in the condensed version of the *Code of Jewish Law.*

1. Just as we are forbidden to enjoy food or drink without a blessing, so we are forbidden to enjoy a fragrant odor without saying a blessing, as it is written (*Psalms 150:6*): 'Let everything that has breath praise God.' And what is it that only the soul and not the body derives pleasure thereof? It is the fragrant odor. However, after having enjoyed the fragrance, we are not required to say a concluding blessing, for as soon as we have ceased to inhale it, our pleasure has ceased, and it is akin to food which has already been digested.

2. What blessing do we say over a pleasant odor? If it comes from a vegetable that is fit for food, even if it can be eaten only when mixed with other ingredients, such as the nutmeg or the lemon or the citron, inasmuch as that fruit is used principally as food, we say the blessing 'who has given' (*asher natan*). Some versions read 'who gives (*hanoten*) fragrance into the fruit.' This blessing is said, however, only when we intentionally inhale the fragrance. If when partaking of the fruit, its fragrance has reached us unintentionally, we are not obliged to say the blessing. If we scent roasted coffee which has a pleasant odor, we say the blessing: 'who has given fragrance into fruit.'

3. If the thing out of which the fragrance arises is a tree or plant, we say the blessing: 'Who has created fragrant woods.' Therefore, we say the blessing 'Who has created fragrant woods' over the myrtle, the rose, frankincense, or the like since they are valued chiefly for their fragrance and not as a food. One should not scent pepper or ginger, because authorities disagree about whether or not a blessing should be recited over their odor.

4. If the fragrance arises from grass or herbs, we say the blessing: 'Who has created fragrant herbs.' An herb is distinguished from a tree in the following manner: if it possesses a stem as hard as the stalk of the flax, and is perennial and produces leaves, it is a tree, but if the stalk is always soft, it is merely an herb.

5. If, like the musk, it is neither a tree nor an herb, we say the blessing 'Who has created various kinds of spices' on inhaling its fragrance. It seems to me that the same blessing is to be said on smelling dried mushrooms, if we find their odor pleasant.

6. The special blessing: 'Who has created sweet-scented oil,' has been instituted over balsam oil, which grows in the land of Israel, on account of its special association with the land of Israel.

7. If we are in doubt as to what blessing to say because we are unable to distinguish the species, we should say the blessing 'Who has created various kinds of spices.'

8. Oil or wine that has been spiced with fragrant wood, is subject to the blessing 'Who has created fragrant woods,' and if spiced with fragrant plants, it is subject to the blessing 'Who has created fragrant herbs.' If spiced with both, it is subject to the blessing: 'Who has created various kinds of spices.'

9. If fragrant fruit, odorous wood, plants, and spices are set before us, we should say the blessing appropriate to each in the following order: first over fruit, then over the wood, the plants, and the spices.

10. Wherever the spices are not meant for the special purpose of smelling them, such as spices stored in a room as merchandise, and perfume used only to scent garments and not meant to be inhaled for its fragrance, these spices and perfumes require no blessing, even when we smell them intentionally. If however, we enter a store where various spices are sold, or a chemist's shop, and we intend to smell them, we should previously say the blessing 'Who has created various kinds of spices,' as the spices are placed there for this purpose as a means of attracting customers.

11. When the scent arises from an object other than the original source, as from fumigated garments, or from a vessel that had contained

spices, or from hands, after handling citrons or other fragrant fruit, no blessing is required.

BLESSINGS RELATED TO SIGHTS
AND SOUNDS IN NATURE

Psalm 19 says that the heavens declare the glory of God. Natural phenomena have always moved the pious Jew to praise and thank God for the wondrous sights and sounds and beauty of nature. There are also blessings on the occasion of seeing scholars, kings, or persons whose physical traits are varied, such as a very tall person or a dwarf. Following are the blessings in gratitude of the gift of sight and sound.

BLESSING ON SEEING WONDERS OF NATURE (LIGHTNING, SHOOTING STARS, HIGH MOUNTAINS, OR SUNRISE)
Praised are You, Lord our God, Ruler of the Universe, Source of Creation.

BLESSING ON HEARING THUNDER OR SEEING A STORM
Praised are You, Lord our God, Ruler of the Universe, whose power and might fill the entire world.

BLESSING ON SEEING A RAINBOW
Praised are You, Lord our God, Ruler of the Universe, who remembers His covenant, is faithful to it, and keeps His promise.

BLESSING ON SEEING TREES BLOSSOMING FOR THE FIRST TIME IN THE YEAR
Praised are You, Lord our God, Ruler of the Universe, who has withheld nothing from His world and who has created beautiful creatures and beautiful trees for people to enjoy.

BLESSING ON SEEING THE OCEAN
Praised are You, Lord our God, Ruler of the Universe, who has made the great sea.

BLESSING ON SEEING TREES OR CREATURES OF STRIKING BEAUTY
Praised are You, Lord our God, Ruler of the Universe, who has such beauty in His world.

LAWS OF BLESSINGS RELATED TO
SIGHTS AND SOUNDS IN NATURE

Following is a synopsis of the laws related to blessings over sights and
sounds in nature as culled from the condensed version of the *Code
of Jewish Law*.

1. On seeing fruit trees blossom, one must say the blessing: Praised
   are You, Lord our God, Sovereign of the Universe, who has made
   the world wanting in naught, but has produced therein goodly
   creatures and goodly trees wherewith to give delight to the children
   of men. This blessing should be said only once a year. If one delayed
   saying the blessing until the fruit grew, one should no longer say
   it. Some authorities hold that if one neglected to say the blessing
   upon seeing the blossom for the first time, one should no longer
   say it.

2. On seeing shooting stars that dart across the sky with a transient
   light, or a comet, or a meteor, or on witnessing an earthquake, or a
   hurricane, or lightning, we say the blessing: Praised are You, Lord
   our God, Sovereign of the Universe, who has made the work of
   creation. This blessing should be said over a shooting star but once
   during the night, even if we see more than one. Over a comet we
   say a blessing but once in thirty days. On hearing thunder after the
   lightning has flashed, we say the blessing: Praised are You, Lord
   our God, Ruler of the Universe, whose strength and might fill the
   world. If we see lightning and hear thunder simultaneously, we say
   the blessing: Who has made the creation.

3. On seeing the rainbow, we say the blessing: Praised are You, Lord
   our God, Sovereign of the Universe, who remembers His covenant,
   is faithful to His covenant, and keeps His promise. We must not
   gaze at the rainbow too much.

4. At the sight of seas, or mountains famous for their great height, we
   say the blessing: Who has made the work of creation.

5. On seeing goodly trees or beautiful creatures, whether human or
   animal, we say the blessing: Praised are You, Lord our God, Ruler
   of the Universe, who has such as this in His world. This blessing

is to be said only upon seeing them the first time, and need not be repeated on seeing them again or even others of the same kind, unless the latter are more beautiful than the former.

6. On seeing the sun at the end of its cycle, that is, after a period of twenty eight years, when the vernal equinox of the month *Nisan* begins, at the approach of nightfall on the eve of the fourth day, we say on the morning of the fourth day after sunrise, the blessing 'who has made the work of creation'.

7. If the Holy One, blessed be He, has wrought a miracle for someone, having saved him in a supernatural way, then on seeing the place where the miracle occurred, one says the blessing: Praised are You, Lord our God, Ruler of the Universe, who has wrought a miracle for me in this place.

8. On seeing a great Jewish scholar, distinguished for their knowledge of the *Torah*, one says the blessing: Praised are You, Lord our God, Ruler of the Universe, who has imparted of His wisdom to them that fear Him. On seeing a person, distinguished in secular knowledge, one says: Praised are You, Lord our God, Ruler of the Universe, who has given of His wisdom to flesh and blood.

9. On seeing a sovereign of any of the nations of the world, we say the benediction: Praised are You, Lord our God, Ruler of the universe, who has given of His glory to flesh and blood. Even if we do not see the ruler in person, but witness the pomp and ceremony and we are certain of the ruler's presence, we may say this blessing.

10. On seeing graves of Israelites we say: Praised are You, O Lord our God, Ruler of the Universe, who has formed you in judgement.

11. On seeing an unusual creature: Praised are You, Lord our God, Ruler of the universe, who varies the forms of His creatures.

Birkat Hagomel: Blessing of Deliverance

Persons who have safely returned from some hazardous voyage, recovered from a serious illness, or been released from unjust imprisonment, have an opportunity to express gratitude to God in the form of a blessing that is recited in addition to the Torah blessings when they are called to the public reading of the Torah in the synagogue. This blessing is known as *birkat hagomel* and is derived from *Psalm 107* according to the Talmudic tractate of *Berachot 54b*. *Psalm 107* begins by calling upon exiles who were brought back to their homes to give thanks. It then describes God's goodness in taking care of lost travelers, prisoners, the sick, and sea voyagers. The refrain at the end of each of the four stanzas reads: 'Let them thank God for His kindness and His wonders toward people.' As a mnemonic, the four letters of the Hebrew word *chayim* have been suggested as the initials of *choli* (illness), *yisureen* (torture), *yam* (sea) and *midbar* (desert).

The *birkat hagomel* is said in the presence of a *minyan* (ten adults). In this way, the person who has safely returned from a journey or recovers from an illness publicly acknowledges his or her gratitude to God in the presence of the community. The *birkat hagomel* blessing reads as follows: Praised are You, Lord our God, Sovereign of the universe, who bestows favors on the undeserving for having shown me every goodness.

Those who hear this blessing respond as follows:

May He who bestowed every goodness upon you, continue to bestow every goodness upon you forever.

The custom today is for a person to say *birkat hagomel* when called to the *Torah* for an *aliyah*. It is said aloud immediately after the second *Torah* blessing. Traditional women have been known to say the blessing after childbirth.

LAWS OF BIRKAT HAGOMEL

Following are some of the laws and customs related to the *birkat hagomel* as culled from the condensed version of the *Code of Jewish Law*.

1. A person must thank God for special mercy (that is, one must say the blessing *hagomel*):

    - on crossing the ocean and reaching the desired destination
    - on crossing safely the desert or any dangerous road, or on being saved from any peril, as when a wall collapsed upon them, or an ox attempted to gore them, or robbers attacked them
    - on recovering from a serious illness, or from a serious wound, or from any illness which has confined them to bed for at least three days
    - on being released from prison, even if the imprisonment was due to civil matters.

    All these should say the blessing, 'Praised are You, Lord our God, King of the Universe, who vouchsafes benefits to the undeserving, who has vouchsafed all good to me,' to which the listeners respond: 'He who has vouchsafed all good to you, may He vouchsafe all good unto you forever.'

2. The blessing *Hagomel* should be said in the presence of no less than ten people, in addition to the one saying the blessing. Two of the ten should be scholars who are engaged in the study of the *Torah*, as it is written (*Psalms 107:32*): 'Let them exalt Him also in the assembly of the people, and praise Him in the seat of the elders.' But if no scholars are available, it should not deter a person from

saying the blessing. It is customary to say this blessing on being called to the reading of the *Torah*.

3. A person for whom a miracle was wrought should set aside a certain sum of money for charity as much as their means will allow. One should divide it among people who are engaged in the study of *Torah*, and say: 'Behold, I give this money to charity, and may it be the Divine will to count it as if I had brought a thanksgiving offering.' It is also fitting that one shall establish some community project in town, and every year on the anniversary, to thank God, and recount the miracle.

4. If one sneezes, we say to them *livriyut* (To your good health) whereupon they respond *Baruch Atah* (Blessed be you).

Sabbath and Festival Blessings

SABBATH

The Jewish Sabbath, which begins with sunset on Friday evening and ends with darkness on Saturday evening, presents those who observe it with an opportunity to rest mind and body, and to express appreciation for many of the things which they are often too busy to notice during the week. The Sabbath itself dates back to the beginning of creation. The Bible relates that God made the world in six days, and on the seventh day God rested, blessing the day, and making it holy. Jewish families do the same in a series of rituals that invoke blessings. Following are the Sabbath blessings:

Birkat HaNerot (Blessing of Lights)

The lighting of Sabbath candles traditionally was the special duty of the housewife ever since ancient times. (*Mishnah Shabbat 2:6*). Jewish tradition permits a man to perform this ritual if there is no woman present. Though there is no biblical command concerning the Sabbath lights, the blessing is worded 'Praised are You who has commanded us to light the Sabbath lights.' This is in keeping with the command: 'You shall carry out the directions that the sages give you.

A beautiful Jewish legend tells of Adam, the first man, who opened his eyes on the eve of the Sabbath. He found himself in the beautiful Garden of Eden, and the sun was shining. But as the sun began to set, Adam became afraid, never having seen the shadows all around him. He thought that the world was coming to an end. Suddenly Adam stumbled upon two stones. He picked them up and struck them together. A spark jumped out and a fire was lit in the grass. Adam looked at the fire and felt how warm it was, a gift from God. It was then that Adam spoke the very first *berachah*, the first blessing ever heard on earth: 'Praised are You, Lord our God, Sovereign of the Universe, who creates the light of the fire.'

The blessing for lighting the candles is not quoted in the *Talmud*, but is found in the ninth century prayerbook of Rav Amram Gaon. The custom of lighting a minimum of two lights, then adding one for each of the remaining members of the household, alludes to the two words 'Remember' and 'Observe', which introduce the Sabbath commandment in the Ten Commandments (*Exodus 20:8; Deuteronomy 5:12*). The lights are symbolic of the cheerfulness and serenity which distinguish the Sabbath as a day of delight. The same applies to all holy days.

It is customary for the woman to cover her eyes while reciting the blessing at the lighting of the Sabbath lights. The reason is that she must not enjoy the Sabbath lights prior to the blessing, in keeping with the rule that the blessing ought to precede the act. When she kindles the festival lights, however, she recites the blessing and then lights the candles. Some people shield their eyes with their hands as soon as they light the candles. Others precede this gesture by making three circular hand motions over the candles, as though to draw the Sabbath into the home.

Here is the Sabbath candle lighting blessing:

Praised are You, Lord our God, Ruler of the Universe, who has sanctified us by His commandments and commanded us to kindle the Sabbath [and festival] lights.

Birkat Hamishpacha (Family Blessing)

The blessing of children by their parents on all important occasions, notably on the eves of Sabbaths and festivals, is hailed as one of Judaism's most beautiful customs. The *Brandspiegel*, a medieval treatise on morals (published in 1602), speaks of this practice in these terms: 'Before the children can walk they should be carried on Sabbaths and festivals to the father and mother to be blessed; after they are able to walk they shall go of their own accord with bowed body and shall incline their heads to receive the blessing. This custom has linked the generations together in mutual loyalty and affection.'

The Jewish people have always ascribed great importance to parental blessings. Added significance was attached to the blessing given by a dying parent in the biblical and Talmudic periods.

The blessing for boys invokes the shining examples of Jacob's grandchildren Ephraim and Manasseh, who did not lose their identity as Jews, even though they were raised in Egypt. The blessing for girls refers to the four matriarchs Sarah, Rebekah, Rachel, and Leah, all of whom were known for their concern and compassion for others.

It is customary for parents is to bless their children before sitting down to the festive meal. This provides them with a privileged opportunity to express appreciation for their children – something they may not always have the leisure to do during the busy and hectic week. Through the touch of a parent's hands or the sound of a parent's voice, children can feel and respond to the love and affection their family has for them.

The blessing is as follows:

FOR SONS: May God give you the blessings of Ephraim and Menasseh

FOR DAUGHTERS: May God give you the blessings of Sarah, Rebekah, Rachel, and Leah.

CONTINUE FOR ALL: May God bless you and guard you. May God show you favor and be gracious to you. May God show you kindness and grant you peace.

Sabbath *Kiddush* (Blessing Over Wine)

Because joy and happiness are synonymous with the Sabbath, it has become customary to begin the meal by reciting the *kiddush*, the blessing over the wine. The *kiddush*, an act of sanctification, is performed on the eve of every Jewish festival as well. In the *kiddush* we thank God for having created the grapes from which wine is made. We also thank God for creating the world and giving us the holy *Shabbat*.

Although it is traditional for the father to recite the kiddush on behalf of the household, women may do it as well. The person who officiates stands up, and in most families those gathered around the table rise as well during the recitation. Family members and guests are each given a cup of wine, which they hold in one hand. The leader then recites the following, alone or joined by the others.

> Praised are You, Lord our God, Ruler of the Universe, who creates the fruit of the vine. Praised are You, Lord our God, Ruler of the Universe, whose *mitzvot* add holiness to our lives, cherishing us through the gift of His holy Shabbat granted lovingly, gladly, a reminder of Creation. It is the first among our days of sacred assembly which recall the Exodus from Egypt. Thus, You have chosen us, endowed us with holiness, from among all peoples by granting us Your holy *Shabbat* lovingly and gladly. Praised are You, God, who hallows *Shabbat*.

Netilat Yadayim (Blessing for Hand Washing)

Ritual hand washing follows the recitation of the *kiddush*. Just as the ancient priests cleansed their hands before performing their duties in the Temple, Jews wash their hands to sanctify the act of eating.

Hand washing should be done over the kitchen sink or a large basin. The left hand grasps a cup or a pitcher of water and pours over the right. The process is reversed and repeated once or twice. The following blessing is recited:

> Praised are You, Lord our God, Sovereign of the Universe, who has sanctified us through His commandments and commanded us to wash our hands.

The hands are then dried. It is customary to remain silent from the moment of ritual washing until the blessing over the bread has been recited and a morsel of *challah* is eaten.

Hamotzi (Blessing Over Bread)

The bread that is eaten on the Sabbath and Jewish festivals is usually a braided loaf called *challah*. It is traditional to place two *challot* on the table to recall the double portion of manna God provided for the Israelites in the desert on the sixth day of the week because no manna fell on the Sabbath. A cloth is spread over the challot to symbolize the dew that covered the manna. The covering is removed just before the recitation of the blessing:

Praised are You, Lord our God, Sovereign of the universe, who brings forth bread from the earth.

One loaf is divided among the assembled participants. In some homes, salt is sprinkled on the individual morsels as another reminder of Temple times, when salt was used during the sacrificial rites.

Havdalah (Farewell to the Sabbath)

The ritual conclusion of the Sabbath is deferred until about an hour after sunset, to make the sweetness and the holiness of the day last as long as possible. When three stars are visible in the evening sky, it is time for the Havdalah (separation) ritual. The ceremonial objects used in this ceremony include a *Kiddush* cup set on a plate filled with wine, a spice box containing aromatic spices, such as cloves or cinnamon, and a braided multi-wick candle. The *Havdalah* blessing over the wine sanctifies reentry into the secular world. The blessing over the spices assures that the memory of the Sabbath just gone by will be fragrant and lingering. The blessing over the braided candle which is lit and held by a family member marks the beginning of the new week, since kindling fire was prohibited on the holy Sabbath.

The person who leads the *Havdalah* ritual raises the cup of wine and says:

Praised are You, Lord our God, Ruler of the universe, who creates the fruit of the vine.

Next, he or she lifts the spice box and says:

Praised are You, Lord our God, Ruler of the universe, who creates all kinds of spices.

The leader then sniffs the spices and passes the spice box around for everyone to share in the fragrant smells designed to mitigate the sadness that the departure of the Sabbath instills in us.

The leader then recites the blessing over the candle:

Praised are you, Lord our God, Ruler of the universe, who creates the lights of the fire.

While the above blessing is recited, family members hold out their hands with palms up, cup their hands and look at the reflection of the flame on their fingernails. In this way, they make use of the light. In addition, they see the shadow formed on their palms by their fingers and actually witness the separation between light and darkness.
The final blessing is as follows:

Praised are You, Lord our God, Ruler of the universe who makes a distinction between sacred and secular, light and darkness, Israel and other peoples, the seventh day and the six days of labor. Praised are You, God, who makes a distinction between sacred and secular.

All then take a sip of the wine from the Kiddush cup and the leader pours some of the remaining wine onto the plate and extinguishes the flame of the Havdalah candles by dipping its tip into the wine. The Sabbath is now officially concluded and all wish each other *shavuah tov* – a good week.

FESTIVALS

Festival *Kiddush*

Praised are You, Adonai our God, Ruler of the Universe who creates the fruit of the vine. Praised are You, God, Ruler of the Universe, who has chosen and distinguished us from among all others by adding holiness to our lives with His *mitzvot*. Lovingly You have given us (*Shabbat* for rest and) Festivals for joy and holidays for happiness, among them this (*Shabbat* and this) day of:
Passover, season of our liberation (*said on Passover*)
Shavuot, season of the giving of the Torah (*said on Shavuot*)
Sukkot, season of our joy (*said on Sukkot*)

Shemini Atzeret, season of our joy (*said on Shemini Atzeret*) a day of sacred assembly recalling the Exodus from Egypt. Thus You have chosen us, endowing us with holiness from among all peoples by granting us (*Shabbat* and) Your hallowed Festivals (lovingly and gladly) in happiness and joy. Praised are You, God, who hallows (*Shabbat* and) the people Israel and the Festivals.

Kiddush for Rosh Hashanah

The special blessing over the wine for *Rosh Hashanah* recalls the sounding of the *shofar*, the wake- up call to repentance.

Praised are You, Lord our God Ruler of the Universe who creates fruit of the vine. Praised are You, Lord our God ruler of the Universe who has chosen us from among all others by adding holiness to our lives with His *mitzvot*. Lovingly, have You given us the gift of this Day of Remembrance, a day for recalling the *shofar sound,* a day for sacred assembly recalling the exodus from Egypt. Thus, You have chosen us, endowing us with holiness from among all peoples. Your faithful word endures forever. Praised are You, King of all the earth, who hallows the people Israel and the Day of Remembrance.

Blessing for Sounding the Shofar

The blessing acknowledges the religious obligation to hear the sound of the ram's horn, the call to repentance.

Baruch Ata Adonai Elohaynu melech haolam asher kidshanu bemitzvotav vetzivanu lishmo'ah kol shofar.

Praised are You, Lord our God, Ruler of the Universe who has made us holy by His commandments and commanded us concerning the sounding of the *shofar*.

Blessing on Using a Lulav and Etrog

Waving the *lulav* (palm, willow, and myrtle) while holding the *etrog* (citron) is an integral ceremony to the celebration of the festival of

Sukkot. Waving the *lulav* in all directions symbolizes God's omnipotence. According to Jewish mystics, each element represents a part of the human body, and holding them together is a reminder to worship God with one's entire being.

> *Baruch Ata Adonai Elohaynu melech haolam asher kidshanu bemitzvotav vetzivanu al netilat lulav.*

> Praised are You, Lord our God, Ruler of the Universe who has made us holy by His commandments and commanded concerning the taking of a palm branch.

Blessing on Eating in a Sukkah

The *sukkah* (a booth) commemorates the booths in which the Israelites lived when they left Egypt. Eating (and sometimes sleeping) in the *sukkah* during the festival of *Sukkot* emphasizes the fragility of life.

> *Baruch Ata Adonai Elohaynu melech haolam asher kidshanu bemitzvotav vetzivanu layshev basukkah.*

> Praised are You, Lord our God, Ruler of the Universe who has made us holy by His commandments and commanded us to dwell in the *sukkah.*

Hanukkah Blessings

Hanukkah is celebrated for eight days, commemorating the victory of the Maccabees over the Syrian Greeks. According to Jewish tradition, when the troops entered the desecrated Temple they could find only one cruse of oil, sufficient for only one day. However, a miracle happened and the small quantity of oil burned for eight full days. In commemoration of this happy event, *Hanukkah* is celebrated for eight days. On each night, a candle is lit on the *hanukkiah* (Hanukkah *menorah*) and blessings are recited. Here are the Hanukkah blessings:

> Praised are You, Lord our God, Ruler of the Universe, who has made us holy with commandments and commanded us to light the *Hanukkah* candles.

Praised are You, Lord our God, Ruler of the Universe who accomplished miracles for our ancestors in ancient days and in our time.

On the first night only add: Praised are You, Lord our God, Ruler of the Universe who has kept us alive, sustained us, and enabled us to reach this season.

Blessing for Reading the *Megillah*

The *Megillah* (*Scroll of Esther*) is read on the festival of *Purim*. It recounts the salvation of the Jews in Persia during the reign of King Ahasueros.

Baruch Ata Adonai Elohaynu melech haolam asher kidshanu bemitzvotav vetzivanu al mikra megillah.

Praised are You, Lord our God, Ruler of the Universe who has made us holy by His commandments and commanded us concerning the reading of the *Megillah*.

Blessing for Eating *Matzah* (Unleavened Bread)

Matzah represents the unleavened bread that the Israelites ate when fleeing Egypt.

Baruch Ata Adonai Elohaynu melech haolam asher kidshanu bemitzvotav vetzivanu al acheelat matzah.

Praised are You, Lord our God, Ruler of the Universe who has made us holy by His commandments and commanded us concerning the eating of unleavened bread.

Blessing for Eating *Maror* (Bitter Herbs)

Maror (bitter herbs) symbolizes the harshness of the slavery that the Israelites endured in Egypt.

Baruch Ata Adonai Elohaynu melech haolam asher kidshanu bemitzvotav vetzivanu al acheelat maror.

Praised are You, Lord our God, Ruler of the Universe who has made us holy by His commandments and commanded us concerning the eating of bitter herbs.

Blessing for Counting the *Omer*

The counting of the *Omer* (literally, a sheaf of barley) extends from the second night of Passover for 49 successive days. It recalls the time when Israelites would bring their first sheaves of barley to the Temple as a thanksgiving offering. Counting up from Passover to the festival of *Shavuot* was intended to heighten one's anticipation of *Shavuot,* when the Israelites received the Ten Commandments at Mount Sinai.

Baruch Ata Adonai Elohaynu melech haolam asher kidshanu bemitzvotav vetzivanu al sefirat haomer.

Praised are You, Lord our God, Ruler of the Universe who has made us holy by His commandments and commanded us concerning the counting of the *omer.*

Hallel Blessing

The *Hallel* service is comprised of psalms of praise that are recited on joyous Jewish festivals.

Baruch Ata Adonai Elohaynu melech haolam asher kidshanu bemitzvotav vetzivanu leekro et ha-hallel.

Praised are You, Adonai our God, Ruler of the Universe, who has made us holy by His commandments and commanded us concerning the reciting of *Hallel.*

Blessings for Rites of Passage

Jewish life cycle events such as *brit milah* (circumcision), *pidyon haben* (redemption of the first-born son), *Bar and Bat Mitzvah,* marriage and even death are special family celebrations. There are also special observances for burial and mourning and for when a person becomes Jewish (conversion). Each rite is accompanied by a pageantry of ritual and custom, law and folklore, feasting and celebration. Each rite is intended as an opportunity for families to celebrate, rejoice or mourn with friends, linking them not only to the community of today but to the communities of past generations.

It should not come as a surprise that many of the Jewish life cycle events are accompanied by blessings, in gratitude of the gift of God's commandments to the Jewish people. Following is a brief synopsis of the Jewish life cycle events that contain blessings, beginning with the rite of circumcision.

BRIT MILAH (CIRCUMCISION)

Brit Milah, the covenant of circumcision, is first mentioned in the *Book of Genesis 17:9–12* as a divine command to Abraham. God said to Abraham: 'You shall keep my covenant, you and your descendants after you throughout their generations . . . Every male among you shall be circumcised . . . and it shall be a sign of the covenant between me and you. He that is eight days old shall be circumcised.

According to the Bible, Abraham followed God's command and not only circumcised his male children but even circumcised himself at age ninety-nine! The circumcision became a symbol for Abraham and his male descendants that they would observe God's ways and obey God's commandments. Thus circumcision is Judaism's first rite of passage for boys, performed with prayers and prescribed rules and regulations as a religious spiritual act, not merely as a surgical procedure.

There are several blessings recited at every circumcision. In the first, the *mohel* (person performing the ritual circumcision) recites a blessing before actually performing the circumcision. The blessing is as follows:

> Praised are You, Lord our God, Ruler of the Universe, who has made us holy through His commandments and commanded us concerning circumcision.

The circumcision is then performed. After the circumcision is completed, the father (and often the mother too) recite the following blessing:

> Praised are You, Lord our God, Ruler of the Universe, who has made us holy through His commandments and commanded us to bring our son into the covenant of Abraham our ancestor.

All of those present then respond:

> As he has entered the covenant, so too may he enter a life of Torah, marriage, and good deeds.

The officiant then recites the traditional blessing over a cup of wine, which includes the formal naming of the baby. Following are the blessings that are used for the naming of the baby boy immediately following the circumcision:

> Praised are You, Lord our God, Ruler of the Universe, who has created the fruit of the vine.

> Praised are You, God, Ruler of the Universe, who has sanctified the well-beloved (Isaac) from the womb and has set Your statute in his flesh, and has sealed his offering with the sign of Your holy covenant. Therefore, God, deliver from destruction the dearly

beloved of our flesh, for the sake of the covenant You have set in our bodies. Praised are You, God, who has made the covenant.

PIDYON HABEN (REDEMPTION OF THE FIRSTBORN SON)

The ceremony of redeeming a first born son (*pidyon haben*) on the thirty first day after birth has its origin in *Exodus 13:13* and *Numbers 18:16*. This precept was originally designed to counteract the heathen practice of sacrificing the firstborn, of man or of beast, to the Semitic gods.

The firstborn sons in Israel originally belonged to the service of God. Later, the Levites were chosen to replace the firstborn of all the other tribes for service in connection with the sanctuary. In return for this, every firstborn Israelite was to be redeemed by paying five *shekels* to a *kohen*, descendant of the priestly family belonging to the tribe of Levi.

When the father presents the five *shekels* to the *kohen*, he says the following:

> I want to redeem my son. Here is the equivalent of five *shekels*, and thus I fulfil my obligation according to the Torah.

The *kohen* receives the redemption money, returns the child to his father, whereupon the father (and mother) recites this blessing:

> Praised are You, Lord our God, Ruler of the Universe, who has made us holy by His commandments and commanded us concerning the redemption of the firstborn.

The father and mother then join in saying the special blessing for the gift of life, called the *shehecheyanu*:

> Praised are You, God, Ruler of the Universe who has kept us alive, sustained us and enabled us to reach this day.

After the *kohen* accepts the five *shekels* and declares the boy redeemed, he concludes by placing his hands upon the head of the child and recites the three-fold priestly blessing:

May God make you like Ephraim and Manasseh.
May God bless you and keep you.
May God's Presence shine and be good to you.
May God's face turn toward you and give you peace.

The blessings over the wine and challah are recited, and a festive meal is usually served to the invited guests.

BAR/BAT MITZVAH

The *Talmud* applies the Hebrew term *Bar Mitzvah* to every adult Jew in the sense of 'one who is obligated' by *mitzvot*. In Judaism, a Jewish boy at the age of thirteen (age twelve for girls), reaches religious maturity and is held thereafter personally responsible for their religious acts. This entrance to religious adulthood today is expressed by extending the adult privilege of reading the Torah or being called to the Torah. Traditionally, this occurs the first Sabbath after one's thirteenth/ twelfth birthday. From this time onward the individual is regarded as a Jewish adult in all religious aspects.

In traditional circles, it is customary for the *Bar Mitzvah*'s parents to recite the following blessing:

Blessed be the One who has relieved me of the responsibility of this boy.

This is an expression of the parent's joy that their son has attained an age when he can independently distinguish between right and wrong. The rationale for saying this blessing is that until the children reaches age thirteen, it is the parents' responsibility to see that their son studies *Torah*. From that age onward, the responsibility for keeping this important religious obligation devolves entirely to the son.

THE JEWISH WEDDING

According to Jewish belief, marriage is part of the natural way of life. The Bible says that 'it is not good for man to be alone. I will make a complement for him' (*Genesis 2:18*). The *Talmud* goes on to reiterate that 'any man who has no wife lives without joy, blessing and goodness' (*Talmud Yevamot 62b*).

The first blessing in recorded in history was the one God gave to Adam and Eve, when He blessed them (*Genesis 1:28*). Jewish tradition has created blessings to be recited in the ceremony that binds a Jewish man to a Jewish woman as husband and wife. These blessings are found in the Talmudic tractate *Ketubot 8a*.

The Jewish wedding ceremony itself consists of two sets of blessings. The first is called the Blessing of Betrothal (*Birkat Erusin*) which consists of a single blessing preceded by the traditional blessing over the wine. The second set of wedding blessings, called *shevah berachot* (seven blessings) consists of six blessings which are also preceded by the blessing over the wine. In the *Talmud* these blessings are referred to both as *birkat chatanim* (bridegroom's blessing) as well as the seven wedding blessings (*shevah berachot*).

These blessings are not only recited during the wedding ceremony itself but also after the Grace After Meals (*Birkat HaMazon*) following the wedding reception as well as after the festive meals at the home of the new bride and groom or their friends and relatives during the week following the wedding.

Some brides and grooms follow the custom of calling on friends and relatives to chant each of the seven blessings during the wedding ceremony.

Following is a synopsis of the both the *Birkat Erusin* and the Seven Wedding Blessings.

Birkat Erusin (Betrothal Blessings)

The following are the two blessings of betrothal recited during the wedding ceremony:

> Praised are You, Lord our God, Ruler of the Universe, who creates the fruit of the vine.

> Praised are You, Lord our God, Ruler of the Universe who has sanctified us with His commandments and has commanded us

concerning illicit relations; and has prohibited us those who are merely betrothed. But has permitted us to use those lawfully married to us by *chuppah* and *kiddushin*. Praised are You, God, who has sanctified His people Israel by *chuppah* and *kiddushin*.

Two cups of wine are used for the two blessings over wine during the wedding ceremony. In ancient times, the betrothal took place in the bride's home and the nuptials in the groom's (at different times). The two separate blessings over two cups of wine recall that history.

The first blessing of the *Erusin* ceremony is over wine. Wine is Judaism's most festive beverage, and is associated with rejoicing and song. Thus, the first blessing of the wedding ceremony praises God for having created the fruit of the vine.

The second blessing of the Erusin ceremony relates to the sanctity of marriage and the laws concerning illicit relations. Beginning at the moment of betrothal (*Erusin*), the incest laws are extended to include a mate's relatives. Thus the reference to illicit relations emphasizes the new limitations that are connected to the new status of betrothal.

The groom and bride share the first cup of wine after recitation of the second blessing.

Shevah Berachot (Seven Wedding Blessings)

After the groom gives his bride-to-be the marriage ring and the officiant reads and delivers the *ketubah* (marriage contract) to the bride, the officiant (the rabbi and/or cantor, or others who may be given the honor) recite the seven blessings under the *chuppah* (marriage canopy).

The blessings cover a plethora of themes – the creation of the world and of humanity, the survival of the Jewish people, the couple's happiness and the raising of the family. The blessings also put the state of marriage into a relationship with both the beginning of history (the Garden of Eden) and the end of history, with the expectation of the coming of the Messiah.

The seven wedding blessings are as follows:

1. Praised are You, Lord our God, Ruler of the Universe, who has created the fruit of the vine.

2. Praised are You, Lord our God, Ruler of the Universe, who has created all things for His glory.

3. Praised are You, Lord our God, Ruler of the Universe, creator of human beings.

4. Praised are You, Lord our God, Ruler of the universe who has made humans in His image after His likeness, and has prepared, out of his very self, a perpetual fabric.

5. May Zion rejoice as her children are restored to her in joy. Praised are You, O God, who causes Zion to rejoice at her children's return.

6. Grant perfect joy to these loving companions, as You did to the first man and woman in the Garden of Eden. Praised are You, God, who causes Zion to rejoice at her children's return.

7. Praised are You, Lord our God, Ruler of the Universe, who created joy and gladness, bride and groom, mirth, song, delight and rejoicing, love and harmony, peace, and companionship. O Lord our God, may there ever be heard in the cities of Judah and in the streets of Jerusalem voices of joy and gladness, voices of bride and groom, the jubilant voices of those joined in marriage under the bridal canopy, the voices of young people feasting and singing. Praised are You, O God, who causes the groom to rejoice with his bride.

As with the *Erusin* blessings, the *Shevah Berachot* begins with the blessing of the wine. It begins the seven wedding blessings on a festive note with the association of wine at all joyous occasions.

The second wedding blessing is a tribute to God, stating that all things are created for God's glory. The prophet Isaiah once stated (*Isaiah 43:7*) that 'everyone who is called by My (i.e. God's) name, I have created, formed and made for My glory.' The *Midrash* records that God appointed angelic messengers for Adam and brought ornaments for Eve at their wedding, and that God arranged seven wedding canopies set up in Paradise, on which the rabbis of old patterned the seven wedding blessings. Thus the wedding is the time to express gratitude for God's greatness.

The third wedding blessing praises God for having created human beings.

The fourth blessing is an extension of the third. It refers to the perpetual renewal of the human being in the divine form. In this wedding blessing, gratitude is expressed to God for having created man in His image. Image is generally understood by the rabbis to mean that human beings are alone among human beings gifted, like their Creator, with moral freedom and will, and the ability to discern right from wrong. The blessing also states that God created man and woman, fusing them together into a perpetual fabric so that together they might perpetuate life.

The fifth blessing is in consonance with the passage from the Bible that has become Judaism's oath of allegiance to the holy city of Jerusalem: 'If I forget you, O Jerusalem, let my right hand forget its cunning. Let my tongue cleave to the roof of my mouth, if I remember you not, if I set not Jerusalem at the top of my joy.' (*Psalms 137:5–6*). The fifth wedding blessing petitions God to return His children to Zion in joy. Interestingly, the Prophet Isaiah too used the rejoicing of the groom toward the bride as a metaphor to describe the way in which God will rejoice over Jerusalem when God brings the redemption: 'As the bridegroom rejoices over the bride, so shall your God rejoice over you' (*Jerusalem Talmud*).

The sixth blessing expresses the insight that a bride and groom ought to be *re'im ahuvim* --loving companions and best friends. Studies of successfully married couples have shown that couples who continue to maintain a close friendship with one another tend to have lasting marriages.

The seventh and final wedding blessing is the climax of the rejoicing. A series of Hebrew words, each a synonym for joy, are mentioned in this blessing. Gratitude is expressed to God for having created these qualities which contribute to the ultimate happiness of a couple: joy, gladness, mirth, song, delight, rejoicing, love, harmony, peace, and companionship. There is also a reference to the jubilation heard in the streets of Jerusalem at the joy of the bride and groom.

Following the seventh wedding blessing the bride and groom then sip from the second cup of wine.

When the seven wedding blessings are recited at the end of the festive meal following the marriage ceremony, two cups of wine are used. One cup of wine is held by the person leading the Grace after the meal. When they finish leading the Grace, they set the cup down and lift up a second cup as they recite the six basic marriage blessings. This is followed by the recitation of the blessing over the wine over the first cup of wine. Inasmuch as the wine blessing is made for both cups of wine, the wine from the two cups are then mixed together.

Conversion

It is estimated that over ten thousand persons convert to Judaism in the United States each year.

For an adult to convert to Judaism, the traditional requirement is Judaic training under the guidance of a rabbi who becomes the prospective convert's sponsor. It is likely that the candidate will be asked to participate in formal classes and/or private sessions, learning Hebrew, Jewish history, customs and ceremonies and life cycle events.

When the rabbi is satisfied that the prospective convert is knowledgeable enough about Judaism and sincere about living a Jewish life, the final step is taken. Arrangements are made by the rabbi for the candidate to go before a *Bet Din* (a tribunal of three rabbis). The tribunal usually convenes at a place where there is a *mikvah* (ritual bath).

If the candidate is male, he must be ritually circumcised before attending the appointment with the rabbinic tribunal (according to Jewish law). If he has already been circumcised, as is quite common today, then he must undergo a symbolic circumcision, which consists of shedding a drop of blood.

The circumcision (or symbolic circumcision) is performed by a *mohel* (ritual circumciser) who recites these two special blessings:

Praised are You, Lord our God, who has made us holy by His commandments and commanded us to circumcise converts.

Praised are You, God, who has made us holy with commandments and commanded us to circumcise the converts and to shed a drop of blood from the blood of the covenant. For were it not for the blood of the covenant, heaven and earth would not exist. As it is said: Were it not for My covenant daily and nightly, the rules of heaven and earth I could not set. Praised are You, God, Creator of the covenant.

Upon arriving at the *mikveh* (ritual bath), members of the *Bet Din* (rabbinic tribunal) ask the candidate a variety of questions. When the members of the tribunal agree that the conversion candidate has 'passed the test', he or she invited to immerse in the *mikveh*. Following the immersion, the candidate recites the following two blessings:

Praised are You, Lord our God, Ruler of the universe, who has made us holy by His commandments and commanded us concerning ritual immersion.

Praised are You, Lord our God, who has kept us in life and sustained us, and enabled us to reach this occasion.

A short ceremony follows the immersion during which the members of the *Bet Din* sign the document of conversion.

Death and Dying

Just as there is a Jewish way of life, so too there is a Jewish way of death. Over the centuries the rabbis have designed a pattern of practices and rituals which are concerned with every aspect of death. These laws and practices are based upon concern for the emotional and spiritual well-being of the mourner and the honor and respect due to the deceased.

In traditional circles when death comes in the presence of loved ones, the eyes and mouth of the deceased are closed and the body covered with a sheet. This is an act of respect to the departed. Then those present recite the traditional phrase *Baruch Dayan Ha'emet* – Praised be the Righteous Judge.

The *keriah* is the tear made on the mourner's clothing (or a black ribbon attached to the clothing) as an outward sign of grief and mourning and an acceptance of death. The custom originated with biblical heroes such as Jacob, David, and Job, all of whom cut their clothing when learning of the death of a loved one. For example, upon hearing of the death of his son Absalom, King David arose and rent his garments (*II Samuel* 13:21). *Keriah* is one of the most striking Jewish expressions of grief, often performed by the mourner immediately before the funeral service. The rending is an opportunity for psychological relief, allowing the mourner to express anguish and anger by means of an act of self-destruction made sacred by Jewish tradition. *Keriah* is performed while standing.

Keriah is customarily performed on the left side (closest to the heart) for a deceased parent, and on the right side for all others. The following blessing is recited by the mourner immediately before *keriah*:

Praised are You, Lord our God, You are the True Judge.

Much like the Mourner's *Kaddish*, this blessing is a reaffirmation of one's faith in God and in the worthwhileness of life, even during a time of great sorrow. It also recognizes God as the final judge of all humanity.

Blessings in Rabbinic Writings

There are a plethora of rabbinic legends related to blessings and their many uses and nuances. Here are a variety of legends related to the importance of blessings in Jewish life. Each legend will be briefly introduced to help set it into its proper context.

THE BLESSING OF RABBI ISAAC

This legend relates to an incident in the life of two rabbinic sages – Rabbi Nachman and Rabbi Isaac, and a blessing which Rabbi Isaac bestows upon Reb Nachman.

Rabbi Nachman and Rabbi Isaac once were dining together, and Rabbi Nachman said to Rabbi Isaac, 'Let the master expound something.' Rabbi Isaac replied, 'Rabbi Yochanan said the following: One should not converse while eating, lest the windpipe open before the gullet and thus endanger life.' After they had dined, Rabbi Isaac said, 'Thus declared Rabbi Yochanan: Jacob our patriarch is not dead.' Rabbi Nachman objected: 'Was it then for naught that mourners mourned, embalmers embalmed, and gravediggers dug a grave?' Rabbi Isaac replied, 'I derive this teaching from the Bible, where it is said, 'Therefore do not be afraid, O Jacob, My servant, for lo, I will save you from afar, and your seed from the land of their captivity' (*Jeremiah 30:10*). Here the verse compares Jacob to his seed (Israel) – as his seed is alive, so too, he is alive.'

When Rabbi Nachman was about to take leave of Rabbi Isaac, he said, 'Please, Master, bless me.' Rabbi Isaac replied, 'Let me tell you a parable of a man who was traveling in the desert. He was hungry, tired, and thirsty, and he lighted upon a tree whose fruits were delicious and its shade pleasant, and a stream of water was flowing beneath it. He ate of its fruits, drank water from the stream, and rested under the tree's shade. When he was about to continue his journey, he said: Tree, O tree, what blessing shall I give you? If I say to you, 'May your fruits be delicious,' behold, they are delicious. If I say, 'May your shade be pleasant,' behold, it is pleasant. If I say, 'May a stream of water flow beneath you,' behold, a stream of water does flow beneath you. Therefore I say, 'May it be God's desire that all the seedlings taken from you be like you.'

So you, too, Nachman, what blessing shall I bestow upon you? Knowledge of Torah? Behold, you already possess such knowledge. Eminence? You are already eminent. Honor? You are already honored. Riches? You are already rich. Children? You already have children. Therefore I say, 'May it be God's will that your offspring be like you' (*Talmud Taanit 5b–6a*).'

THE BLESSINGS OF RABBI PAPA AND RAV HUNA

The following tale deals with the blessings that Rabbis Papa and Huna recited when they met the very scholarly Rabbi Hanina.

Rabbi Papa and Rabbi Huna son of Rabbi Joshua were once walking along the road when they met Rabbi Hanina son of Rabbi Ika. They said to him: 'The minute we saw you we recited two blessings: 'Blessed be the One who has imparted wisdom to them that fear Him' and 'That has kept us alive.'

He replied: 'And the minute I saw you, I deemed you to be equal to the sixty myriads of the House of Israel, recited three blessings, the two you mentioned and 'Blessed is the One who discerns secrets' (*i.e.*, the blessing spoken at the sight of the hosts of Israel)' (*Talmud Berachot 58b*).

A RIGHTEOUS ONE AND ONE CONDEMNED TO DIE

The following midrashic statement compares the spirituality of a righteous person with that of a person condemned to die, and the likelihood of each to recite blessings.

(Of a person condemned to die, it is said) 'He who is dead shall be put to death' (*Deuteronomy 17:6*), for a wicked man is called dead even while alive, because when he sees the sun shining, he is not stirred to utter in blessing 'Who creates light.' When he sees it set, he is not stirred to say in blessing, 'Who brings on evenings.' When he eats and drinks, he is not stirred to speak a blessing. But the righteous are stirred to bless God for each and everything they eat or drink, or see, or hear (*Tanchuma, Beracha, paragraph 7*).

FIXED VERSUS SPONTANEOUS BLESSINGS

This midrash deals with the question of whether one must use the exact traditional words of a blessing or whether one's own personal spontaneous blessing suffices.

Rabbi Meir said: 'Even if one merely sees a loaf of bread and says, 'Blessed is the One who created this bread; how beautiful is this bread' – that is the same as a blessing over it. Even if he sees figs and says, 'Blessed is the One who created these figs; how beautiful they are' – that is the same as a blessing over them.'

But Rabbi Yose said: 'One who changes the formula that the sages have fixed for blessings has not discharged his duty' (*Tosafot Berachot 4:4–5*).'

THE TALE OF RABBAN GAMALIEL

The following midrashic tale relates to a most interesting incident in the life of Rabban Gamaliel and a blessing that he recited after having seen a gentile woman of beauty.

When a man sees beautiful trees or beautiful people, he should say: 'Blessed be the One who has created such beautiful creatures in God's world.'

It happened once that when Rabban Gamaliel saw a beautiful gentile woman, he uttered a blessing at the sight of her. But was it not said in the name of Rabbi Yochanan that the words 'You shall show them no grace' (*Deuteronomy* 7:2) means 'You shall ascribe no grace to them?'

But what had Rabban Gamaliel said? He did not say *Abaskanta* (Greek for 'May God keep you from harm'). All he said was 'Who has created such beautiful creatures in God's world.' For even if he had seen a beautiful camel, a beautiful horse, a beautiful donkey, he would have said, 'Blessed be the One who has created beautiful creatures in His world.'

Was it Rabban Gamaliel's habit to gaze at women? No, but the road was tortuous and he looked at her without having intended to (*Jerusalem Talmud, Berachot* 9:2).

A POTPOURRI OF BLESSINGS

Following is a rabbinic discussion about a variety of blessings for various occasions, including those over a seeing a crowd of Israelites, sages in Israel, sages of other nations and both Israelite kings and kings of other nations.

If one sees a crowd of Israelites, one is to say 'Blessed is the One who discerns things that are secret' for the mind of each is different from that of every other, just as the face of each is different from that of every other.

Ben Zoma once saw such a crowd on the ascent to the Temple Mount. He said, 'Blessed is the One who discerns things that are secret' and 'Blessed is the One who has created all these people to serve me.' For he used to say 'What effort Adam had to make before he obtained bread to eat. He plowed, he sowed, he reaped, he bound the sheaves, he threshed, he winnowed, and sorted the grain. He ground it and sifted the flour, kneaded, and baked it. And only then, at long last, was he able to eat. Whereas I rise in the morning and find all these things done for me. What effort Adam had to make before he obtained a garment to wear. He had to shear the wool, wash it, comb it, spin it, and weave it. And only then, at long last, did he obtain a garment to wear. Whereas I rise in the morning and find all these things done for me. All kinds of craftsmen come early to the door of my house, and I rise in the morning and find all these necessities before me.'

He used to say 'What does a good guest say? How much trouble my host has gone to for me. How much meat he placed before me and how much wine he brought before me. How many loaves of white bread he set before me? And all the trouble he went to was only for my sake.' But what does a bad guest say? 'How much, in truth, has my host put himself out? I ate only one loaf of bread and ate only one slice of meat, and I drank only one cup of wine. All the trouble my host went to was in fact only for the sake of his wife and children.'

'How according to Bible, does a good guest speak? As notables are sung to, so shall men laud their conduct (*Job 36:24*). But with regard to a bad guest, the Bible says, 'men do therefore shy away from him (*Job 37:24*).'

Our masters taught that on seeing the sages of Israel, one should say 'Blessed is the One who has imparted of His wisdom to them that fear God.' On seeing the sages of other nations, one should say 'Blessed be the One who has imparted of His wisdom to His creatures.' On seeking kings of Israel, one should say 'Blessed is the One who has imparted of His glory to them that fear Him.'

On seeing kings of other nations one should say 'Blessed be the One who has imparted of His glory to His creatures.' (*Talmud Berachot 58a*)

TALE OF ULLA AND RABBI HISDA

This tale deals with a story in the life of Ulla and Rabbi Hisda, and the blessing one says for an inhabited dwelling.

On seeing the houses of Israel, when inhabited one should say 'Blessed be the One who sets up anew the boundaries of the widow (Israel).' If uninhabited 'Blessed be the true Judge.'

Once, when Ulla and Rabbi Hisda were walking along the road, they came to the door of the house of Rabbi Hana bar Hanilai. Rabbi Hisda broke down and sighed. Ulla then said to him, 'Why are your sighing?' Rabbi Hisda answered 'How shall I refrain from sighing on seeing a house in which there used to be sixty cooks by day and sixty cooks by night, who cooked for everyone who was in need. Nor did Rabbi Hana ever take his hand away from his purse, saying to himself: Perhaps a poor man of a good family might come and be put to shame while I reach for my purse. Moreover, the house had four doors opening to the four cardinal points, and whoever came in hungry went out full. In years of scarcity, wheat and barley were placed outside, so that anyone who was ashamed to take some by day could come and take it by night. Now that the house is a mound of ruins, shall I not sigh? (*Talmud Berachot 58b*)'

BLESSING ON SEEING A RAINBOW

This rabbinic tale presents the opinion of Rabbi Joshua ben Levi about which blessing to say upon seeing a rainbow.

Rabbi Joshua ben Levi said 'On seeing the rainbow in the clouds, one should fling himself down upon his face, in keeping with the verse 'At the appearance of the rainbow that is in the cloud … the instant I saw it, I flung myself down upon my face (*Ezekiel 1:28*).' In the west [Land of Israel] they cursed anyone who did this, because it seemed as though he were bowing down to worship the rainbow; but one may certainly say a blessing over it. What blessing should one say? 'Blessed be the One who remembers the covenant, is faithful to God's covenant, and fulfills His promise.'' Rabbi Joshua ben Levi also said: 'One who sees the sky in all of its purity says, 'Blessed be the One who wrought the work of creation.' (*Talmud Berachot 59a*)'

BLESSING FOR RAIN

Rainfall has always been important to the Land of Israel, which has relied so heavily upon its agricultural produce. Following is a rabbinic discussion on the blessing for rain.

When do we begin to say the blessing for rain? When the bridegroom goes out to meet his bride (*i.e.*, when raindrops first strike the earth). What blessing should one say? Rabbi Judah taught: 'We give thanks to You for every drop You caused to fall on us.' Rabbi Yochanan used to conclude the blessing in this way:

> Were our mouths filled with song as the sea is with water
> And our tongue with praise as the roaring waves.
> Were our lips full of adoration
> As the wide expanse of heaven,
> And our eyes sparkling like the sun or the moon.
> Were our hands spread out in prayer as eagles' wings in the sky,
> And our feet as swift as the deer.
> We would still be unable to thank You enough, O God.
> Praised be You, God, to whom thanksgivings are due (*Talmud Berachot 59b*).

BLESSING OVER THE STATUE OF MERCURY

This rabbinic story relates to blessings over the statue of Mercury and the wicked Babylon, arch-enemy of the Israelites.

Our masters taught: 'One who sees a statue of Mercury should say 'Blessed is the One who shows long suffering to those who transgress God's will.' One who sees a place from which idolatry has been uprooted should say 'Blessed be the One who has uprooted idolatry from our Land; and as it has been uprooted from all places where Israel dwell and may You turn the hearts of those that serve them to serve You.''

Rabbi Hamnuna said in a discourse: 'If one gazes upon wicked Babylon, one should say five blessings. On seeing the ruins of Babylon, one should say 'Blessed be the One who has destroyed wicked Babylon.' On seeing the ruins of the palace of Nebuchadnezzar, one should say 'Blessed be the One who destroyed the palace of wicked Nebuchadnezzar.' On seeing the fiery furnace or the lions' den, one should say 'Blessed be the One who wrought miracles for our ancestors in this place.' On seeing the statue of Mercury, one should say 'Blessed be the One who shows long suffering to those that transgress God's will.' On seeing a ruin from which earth is carried away to be used in building, one should say 'Blessed be the One who says and does, who decrees and carries out.'

When Rava would see asses carrying earth, he used to slap them on their back and say, 'Run, righteous ones, to perform the will of your Creator.'

When Mar son of Ravina came to the site of Babylon, he used to pick up some earth in his kerchief and fling it to the wind, to fulfill the text 'I will sweep it with the broom of destruction. (*Isaiah 14:23*).''

BLESSING WHEN SEEING JEWISH GRAVES

In this rabbinic story we learn of the special blessing that one is to say when seeing Jewish graves.

On seeing the graves of Jews, one should say: 'Blessed is the One who fashioned you in justice, who maintained you in justice, fed you in justice, and in justice gathered you in, and in justice will raise you up again.' Mar son of Ravina, citing Rabbi Nachman, used to conclude the blessing in this way:

> And God knows the number of all of you
> And God will bring you back to life and preserve you.
> Blessed be God who brings the dead back to life (*Talmud Berachot 58b*).

RABBI AKIBA AND THE ANGELS' BLESSING

Angels were also believed to recite blessings and act as God's chorus each morning. Following is Rabbi Akiba's analysis of the angels' blessings.

Rabbi Akiva said: 'Every day in the morning an angel opens his mouth and says, 'God reigns, God did reign, and God will reign forever and ever,' until the angel reaches 'Bless you.' When he reaches 'bless you,' there stands up in the firmament a creature of the chariot whose name is Israel and upon whose brow 'Israel' is inscribed. It stands in the middle of the firmament and says, 'Bless you the Lord who should be blessed.' And all the troops of angels above respond, saying, 'Blessed is the Lord who should be blessed forever and ever.'

In the firmament there is one celestial creature on whose brow is the symbol 'truth' when it is day, and thus the angels know that it is day. And 'faithfulness' on its brow in the evening, and thus the angels know that it is night. Each time it says, 'Bless God who should be blessed,' all the troops of angels above respond, 'Blessed is God who should be blessed forever and ever' (*Heichalot*).

FAITHFUL ARE THE WOUNDS OF A FRIEND

The following rabbinic tale is a commentary on the verse in the Book of Proverbs 'Faithful are the wounds of a friend, but the kisses of an enemy are importunate' (Proverbs 27:6).

Rabbi Samuel bar Nachmani said in the name of Rabbi Jonathan: What is signified by the verse 'Faithful are the wounds of a friend, but the kisses of an enemy are importunate?' (*Proverbs 27:6*). Better was the curse that Ahijah the Shilonite uttered against Israel than the blessing the wicked Balaam bestowed upon them. Ahijah the Shilonite cursed them by likening them to a reed. He said to Israel: 'The Lord will strike Israel until it sways like a reed in water' (*1 Kings 14:15*).

What is true of a reed? Because a reed grows in a well-watered area, its stock keeps driving up new shoots. And because its roots are many, even if all the winds of the world come and blow at it, they cannot move it from its place, for it sways to and fro with them. When the winds have subsided, the reed resumes its erect stance. But the wicked Balaam blessed them by comparing them to a cedar, saying of Israel 'As cedars' (*Numbers 24:6*). What is true of a cedar? Because it does not grow up in a well-watered area, its stock does not drive up new shoots and its roots are few. Still, even if all the winds of the world come and blow at it, they cannot move it from its place. If however, the south wind blows at the cedar, it uproots it at once and lays it flat on its face. What's more, because it yields so readily, the reed has the privilege of being used for pens with which to write the books of Torah, Prophets and Writings (*Talmud Taanit 20a*).

RABBI HIYYA, RABBI AND A BLIND PERSON

In this rabbinic tale Rabbi Hiyya and Rabbi encounter a blind person. The tale is an attempt to elucidate the type of respect that one would afford to a person without sight.

Rabbi and Rabbi Hiyya were on a journey, and when they came to a certain town, they said, 'If there is a disciple of the wise here, we shall go and pay our respects to him.' They were told, 'There is one disciple of the wise here, but he is blind.' Rabbi Hiyya said to Rabbi, 'Stay here. You must not lower your patriarchal dignity. I shall go and pay my respects for both of us.' But Rabbi took hold of Rabbi Hiyya and went with him. As they were about to leave that disciple of the wise, he said to them, 'You have paid your respects to one who can be seen but cannot see. May you be granted the privilege of paying your respects to God who sees but cannot be seen.'

Hearing that, Rabbi then said to Rabbi Hiyya, 'And you would have deprived me of such a blessing' (*Talmud Hagigah 5b*).

RABBI SHESHET AND THE BLESSING
IN THE PRESENCE OF A KING

There are many rabbinic tales about Rabbi Sheshet, who was blind. This particular tale answers the question of whether a blind person ought to recite a blessing in the presence of a king, even though he cannot see him.

Rav Sheshet was blind. On one occasion, when all the people went out to welcome the king, Rav Sheshet arose and went with them. A certain heretic came across him and said to him, 'Sound pitchers are taken to the river, but why should cracked ones go there?' (*i.e.* Why should a blind person be going to see the king?) Rav Sheshet answered: 'I will show you that I know more than you.'

When the first legion passed by and a shout arose, the heretic said, 'The king is coming,' but Rav Sheshet retorted, 'He has not yet come.' When a second legion passed by, and again a shout arose, the heretic said again, 'The king is coming now,' but Rav Sheshet once more retorted, 'Not yet.'

When a third legion passed by in complete silence, Rav Sheshet said to the heretic, 'Now it is certain that the king is coming.' The heretic asked, 'How do you know this?' Rav Sheshet replied, 'Because royalty on earth is like royalty in heaven, about which it is written, 'God was not in the earthquake, and after the earthquake a still small voice (*1 Kings 19:12*).'

When the king came, Rav Sheshet pronounced the appropriate blessing him. The heretic asked, 'You pronounce a blessing over one you cannot see?' Rav Sheshet fixed his eyes upon him, and sparks of fire came forth and quenched the sight of the heretic's eyes (*Talmud Berachot 58a*).

BAR KAPPARA AND HIS DISCIPLE

This midrash relates an interesting story about recitation of a blessing and the reaction of one who heard it and snickered. The story itself involves Bar Kappara and one of his students who said blessings over various foods, but not in the traditional prescribed order.

Once, while two students were seated before Bar Kappara, cabbage, prunes, and young chickens were set before him. Bar Kappara gave permission to one of the disciples to pronounce the appropriate blessing. When that student in his haste said the blessing over chickens (Note: the proper traditional order would have been a blessing over the prunes, then over the cabbage and lastly over the chickens) his colleague snickered at him.

Bar Kappara became angry and said, 'I am not angry with the one who pronounced the blessing but with the one that snickered. If it appears that your colleague acted like one who has never tasted meat before, what right have you to snicker at him?'

But then Bar Kappara changed his mind and said, 'I am not angry at the one who snickered but I am angry at the one who pronounced the blessing' adding, 'Even if there be no wisdom in me, there is still my seniority' (*Talmud Berachot 39a*).

BLESSING FOR THE ARRIVAL OF THE MESSIAH

This midrash introduces the blessing to be said when the Messiah comes.

Our masters taught: When the King Messiah appears, he will come and stand on the roof of the Temple and make a proclamation to Israel, saying: 'Meek ones, the time of your redemption is come. And if you do not believe me, behold my light, which shines upon you. "Arise, shine, for your light is come, and the glory of God is risen upon you" (*Isaiah 60:1*). And it has risen only upon you and not upon the nations of the earth: "For behold, darkness shall cover the earth, and gross darkness the peoples. But upon you God will arise, and God's glory shall be seen upon you"' (*Isaiah 60:2*).

Then the Holy One will brighten the light of the king Messiah and of Israel, and all the nations shall walk by the light of the Messiah and of Israel: 'And the nations shall walk at your light, and kings at the brightness of your rising' (*Isaiah 60:3*). And they shall all come and lick the dust touched by the feet of the king Messiah. And all of them shall fall down upon their faces before the Messiah and before Israel, and say: Let us be slaves to you and to Israel.'

'As a bridegroom puts on a priestly diadem' (*Isaiah 61:10*). This verse declares that the Holy One will clothe Ephraim, our true Messiah, with a garment whose splendor will radiate from world's end to world's end. And Israel will make use of his light and say:

> Blessed is the hour in which he was created.
> Blessed is the womb whence he came.
> Blessed is the generation whose eyes behold him.
> Blessed is the eye that waits for him, whose lips open with blessing
> and peace.

Whose speech is pure delight, whose heart meditates in trust and
tranquility.
Blessed is the eye that merits seeing him, whose tongue's utterance
is pardon and forgiveness for Israel
Whose prayer is a sweet savor, whose supplication is purity and
holiness.
Fortunate are Israel in what is stored up for them. (*Yalkut, Isaiah
paragraph 499*)

JACOB BLESSES HIS CHILDREN

*This tale explains why Jacob invoked 'God Shaddai' when he blessed his
sons.*

'God *Shaddai* (Almighty) give you mercy' (*Genesis* 43:14). Why did
Jacob invoke 'God *Shaddai*' when he blessed his sons? He used this
name to indicate that more than enough afflictions had come upon
him. While he was yet in his mother's womb, Esau strove with him.
When he fled from Esau to Laban, he spent twenty years there in many
kinds of distress. After he left, Laban pursued him in order to slay him.
As soon as he was delivered from Laban, Esau came and sought to slay
him, and because of Esau he had to give up a huge tribune of cattle
and camels. After he extricated himself from Esau, the distress with
Dinah befell him. After he extricated himself from that distress, there
was the distress of Rachel's death. After such a chain of distress, he
wanted a little repose, but then there befell him the distress of Joseph,
the distress of Simeon, and the distress of Benjamin. That is why Jacob
invoked 'God *Shaddai* (Almighty),' as if to say: May God who said to
heaven and earth, 'Enough (*dai*)' say also to my affliction, 'Enough
(*dai*).' (*Tanchuma Vayigash, paragraph 5*)

'BLESSED BE THE NAME WHOSE GLORIOUS
KINGDOM IS FOREVER AND EVER.'

*This midrash presents the patriarch Jacob's special blessing to his sons as
he lay on his deathbed.*

'And Jacob called to his sons, and said "Gather yourselves together, that I may reveal to you…"' (*Genesis 49:1*). Jacob was about to reveal the time of redemption to his sons, but the Presence left him.

So he said, 'Could it be, God forbid, that my bed has produced an unfit son, as happened to Abraham, my father's father, out of whom sprang Ishmael, or as happened to my father Isaac, out of whom sprang Esau?'

His sons assured him of their steadfastness: 'Hear O Israel (our father), the Lord is our God, the Lord is One' (*Deuteronomy 6:4*). Just as in your heart there is only the One, so in our hearts there is only the One'.

Then our father Jacob pronounced for the first time the blessing 'Blessed be the Name whose glorious kingdom is forever and ever.'

Hence it is reported in the name of Rabbi Samuel – every day, morning and evening, Jews say, 'In the cave of Machpelah where you are at rest, "Hear O Israel (our father)". What you commanded us we still practice: "The Lord is our God; the Lord is One"' (*Talmud Pesachim 56a* and *Genesis Rabbah 98:4*).

ISAAC'S BLESSINGS

The following tale elucidates Isaac's blessing to his sons Esau and Jacob.

'And he called his son Esau' (*Genesis 27:1*). As the nightfall of Passover approached, Isaac called his elder son Esau and said to him, 'My son, on this night the entire world, all of it, sings psalms of praise to God; on this night, the treasuries of beneficent dews are opened. Make me some savory food and I will bless you while I am still in this world.'

To this the Holy Spirit retorted, 'Eat not the bread of one who is up to no good, and desire not his savory morsels' (*Proverbs 23:6*).

Esau went to fetch what Isaac wanted but found himself hindered. Rebekah said to Jacob, 'My son, on this night the treasuries of beneficent dews are opened. On this night angels above utter song. Make some savory food for your father, that he may bless you while he is still in this world.' So Jacob went and fetched two kids of the goats. (*Pirke de Rabbi Eliezer 32*)

THE BLESSING OF JACOB'S ANGEL

Following is the tale about the angelic being with whom Jacob wrestled, and the blessing which Jacob ultimately received.

'And there wrestled a man with him' (*Genesis 32:25*). Some say it was the angel Michael, who said to Jacob, 'If to me, one of the foremost princes in heaven, if to me you have done what you did, why should you be afraid of Esau?'

Rabbi Tarfon said: Michael had no permission to move from the place where he had been wrestling until Jacob gave him leave – for Michael had to beg, 'Let me go, for the day breaks' (*Genesis 32:27*). Jacob retorted, 'Are you a thief or a gambler, that you fear daybreak?'

Just then, many bands of ministering angels came by and said, 'Michael, up with you, for the time of singing God's praise has come'' (*Song of Songs 2:12*). This means: If you do not begin, there will be no morning songs.

Michael began pleading with Jacob, 'I beg you, let me go, lest the ministering angels in *Aravot* (the seventh heaven) incinerate me for delaying the song.' Jacob replied, 'I will not let you go except if you bless me' (*Genesis 32:27*). Michael then asked, 'Who is more beloved, the servitor or the son? I am the servitor and you are the son. Do you require my blessing?'

Jacob answered, 'Nevertheless.' At once Michael said, 'Your name shall no more be called Jacob, but Israel' (*Genesis 32:29*), and went on, 'Blessed are you, born of woman, for you entered the palace above and remained alive' (*Midrash Akvir*).

BLESSING OF MOSES BEFORE HIS DEATH

The following tale is about the blessing that Moses invoked when a divine voice told him that he was about to depart from this world.

A divine voice came forth: 'The moment has come, Moses, for you to depart from this world.' Moses replied, 'Blessed be His Name. May God live and endure forever and forever.' Then Moses said to Israel, 'I implore you, when you enter the Land, remember me and my bones, and say, 'Alas for the son of Amram, who had run before us like a horse, yet his bones fell in the wilderness' (*Deuteronomy Rabbah 7:10 and 11:10*).

BLESSING OF AN ORDINARY MAN

This midrash tells of the blessing of an ordinary man. It is a story of an encounter of Rabbi Ishmael ben Elisha and Akhtariel Yah in the innermost part of the sanctuary.

Rabbi Ishmael ben Elisha said, 'Once when I entered into the innermost part of the sanctuary to offer incense, I saw Aktariel Yah, the Lord of hosts, seated upon a high and exalted throne. He said to me, 'Ishmael, my son, bless Me.' I replied, 'May it be Your will that Your mercy subdue Your wrath and Your mercy prevail over Your other attributes, so that You deal with Your children according to the attribute of mercy; and may You, on their behalf, stop short of the limit of strict justice.' And God nodded His head toward me. Here we learn that the blessing of an ordinary man is not to be regarded lightly in our eyes' (*Talmud Berachot 7a*).

BLESSING OF RABBI SIMEON'S SON

In this tale we learn of the blessing of Rabbi Simeon's son, which Rabbi Simeon did not believe was appropriate. Rabbi Simeon then interprets the blessing for his son.

Rabbi Jonathan ben Akhmai and Rabbi Judah, the son of proselytes, studied the passage on vows at the school of Rabbi Simeon ben Yochai. They had taken leave of him in the evening, but in the morning they came back and took leave of him again. When he asked, 'But did you not take leave of me last night?' they replied, 'Our master, you taught us that a disciple who took leave of his master and then remained to lodge overnight in the city is required to take leave of him once again.'

At this Rabbi Simeon said to his son, 'These men are men of consequence. Go along with them, that they may bless you.'

So the son went to them. When they asked him, 'What do you wish?' he replied, 'My father told me, 'Go along with them, that they may bless you.''

They said to him, 'May it be Heaven's will that you sow but do not reap. That you may bring in but not bring out. That you may bring out but not bring in. That your home remain desolate but your lodging place lived in. That your table be in turmoil and you do not behold a new year.'

When he came home to his father, he said to him, 'Not only did they not bless me – they greatly upset me.' His father asked, 'What did they say to you?' 'They said thus so and so.'

The father: 'Those are indeed all blessings. 'That you sow but do not reap' means that you beget children and they do not die. 'That you bring in but not bring out' means that you bring home daughters-in-law and your sons do not die, so that the wives would be obliged to go back to their father's homes. 'That you bring out but not bring in' means that you give your daughters in marriage and their husbands do not die, so that your daughters are not obliged to come back to you. 'That your home be desolate but your lodging place lived in' – this world is the lodging place and the grave your home. 'That your table be in turmoil' because of many sons and daughters; and 'that you not behold a new year' (with a new wife) – that your wife does not die and you are not obliged to wed a new wife' (*Talmud Moed Katan 9a–b*).

ULLA'S VISIT TO REB NACHMAN

This midrash deals with the permissibility of a woman reciting the blessing over a cup of wine.

Ulla happened to visit the house of Reb Nachman. They had a meal, after which Ulla said grace and then handed the cup of blessing to Reb Nachman to recite the blessing over it. Reb Nachman said to him 'Please send the cup to my wife Yalta, that she may recite it.'

Ulla replied: 'Thus taught Rabbi Yochanan: The fruit of a woman's body is blessed only from the fruit of a man's body, since the Bible says,

'He will also bless the fruit of your body' (*Deuteronomy 7:13*). It does not say, 'The fruit of **her** body,' but 'The fruit of **your** (that is, a man's body'), so if you recite the blessing over the cup, there is no need for her to recite it.' Yalta heard that Ulla had refused to send her the cup, and she flew into a rage, stormed into the wine pantry, and smashed four hundred jugs of wine.

Reb Nachman again said to Ulla, 'Would the master please send her the cup.' Ulla again refused and sent her a message: 'The *nuga* quantity of wine you splattered should provide the cup of blessing you demand.' She shot back the reply, 'Insulting words from itinerant peddlers are as inevitable as vermin from rags' (*Talmud Berachot 51b*).

BLESSING OF RABBI

This midrash describes Rabbi's blessing of thanksgiving to God for a beverage that had been preserved for seventy years in order for it to be effective.

Our masters taught: Once Rabbi, suffering from a pain in his stomach, asked, 'Does anyone know whether a heathen's apple cider is prohibited or permitted?' Rabbi Ishmael son of Rabbi Yose replied, 'My father once had the same complaint, and they brought him a heathen's apple cider which was seventy years old. He drank it and recovered.' Said Rabbi, 'All this time you knew the law as well as the cider's effectiveness, and you let me suffer.'

Upon inquiry, they found a heathen who possessed three hundred kegs of apple cider seventy years old. Rabbi drank some of it and recovered. At that, he exclaimed, 'Blessed be God who is everywhere, who has delivered God's universe into the keeping of those who guard its wellbeing' (*Talmud Avodah Zarah 40b*).

GOD'S BLESSING OF THE SABBATH

This midrash is an interpretation of the biblical verse, 'And God blessed the seventh day' (Genesis 2:3).

'And God blessed the Sabbath day' (*Genesis 2:3*). Rabbi Eleazar said,

'God blessed it by increasing the capacity of the Sabbath lamp, as I myself have experienced. I once lit a lamp for the Sabbath eve, and at the conclusion of the Sabbath I found it still burning and the oil not at all diminished (*Genesis Rabbah 11:2*).

JOURNEY OF RABBI YOCHANAN BEN ZAKKAI AND RABBI ELEAZAR BEN ARAKH

This legend describes the blessing of the trees as Rabbi Eleazar ben Arakh began his exposition of the Work of the Chariot (a highly mystical endeavor only to be studied by the most knowledgeable Jews).

Our masters taught: Once, when on a journey, Rabbi Yochanan ben Zakkai was riding on a donkey and his student Rabbi Eleazar ben Arakh was driving the donkey from behind. Rabbi Eleazar said, 'Master, teach me a chapter in the *Work of the Chariot.*' He answered, 'My son, have I not taught you that the *Work of the Chariot* is not to be taught even to one person, unless he is a sage and able to draw inferences on his own?' Rabbi Eleazar entreated, 'Master, then permit me to say something before you that you already taught me.' He answered, 'Say it.'

Rabban Yochanan ben Zakkai immediately dismounted from his donkey, wrapped his cloak around himself, and sat down on a stone beneath an olive tree. Rabbi Eleazar said to him, 'Why did you dismount from the donkey?' Rabbi Yochanan ben Zakkai answered 'While you are expounding the *Work of the Chariot,* the Divine Presence might be with us, and the ministering angels might accompany us – it is proper that I should continue riding an ass?'

As soon as Rabbi Eleazar ben Arakh began his exposition of the *Work of the Chariot,* fire came down from heaven and lapped at all the trees in the field, which then burst into song. What was the song that they sang? 'Praise God from the earth, you sea monsters and all deeps...fruitful trees and all cedars...*Halleluyah*' (*Psalms 148:7; 148:14*). And an angel was heard from the fire saying, 'Surely this is the very *Work of the Chariot*' (*Talmud Hagigah 14b*).

BLESSING OVER READING THE TORAH

This midrash illustrates the scriptural inference by which it was concluded that a blessing is required over the reading of the Torah.

How do we know that a blessing is to be spoken over the reading of the Torah? Rabbi Ishmael said, 'By inference. If a blessing must be pronounced over an occasion that brings temporal life, all the more so by far over the reading of the Torah, which brings eternal life' (*Talmud Berachot 48b*).

REJOICING AT THE PLACE OF
THE WATER DRAWING

This rabbinic tale describes the blessings recited at the celebration on Sukkot.

He who has not seen the rejoicing at the place of the water drawing has never in his life seen true rejoicing. At the conclusion of the first day of Sukkot, the priests and the Levites went down to the Women's Court, where they put up an elaborate structure to separate men from women. In the Women's Court were also installed golden lampstands, each with four golden bowls at its top. Each lampstand had four ladders by which four novices of the priesthood, holding jars of oil, each jar containing one hundred and twenty log, were able to ascend to its top and pour oil into each of its bowls. The wicks used by the novices to kindle the lamps were made out of priests' worn out undergarments and sashes, which they tore into strips. So abundant was the light that there was no courtyard in Jerusalem that was not illuminated by the light coming from the place of the water drawing.

With burning torches in their hands, men of piety and good deeds used to dance in front of the people, singing songs and praises. And Levites without numbers, with harps, lyres, cymbals, trumpets, and other musical instruments, were there on the fifteen steps leading down from the court of the Israelites to the Court of the Women. It was on these steps that the Levites stood with their musical instruments and played their music. When they reached the floor of the

Women's Court, they sounded a *tekiah*, a *teruah* and a *tekiah*. They proceeded, sounding their trumpets, until they reached the gate that leads out to the east. When they reached that gate, they turned their faces from east to west (toward the Temple) and proclaimed "In the days of the First Temple, our forebears who were in this place stood with their backs toward the Temple of God, their faces to the east, and they bowed low to the sun in the east. But we, our eyes turned to God.' Rabbi Judah said, 'They used to repeat the last words and when they separated one from the other, what did they say to one another? 'The Lord bless you out of Zion: and see you the good of Jerusalem all the days of your life; and see your children's children. Peace be upon Israel'" (*Psalms 128:5–6*).

Blessings, Curiosities
and Customs

Following are some interesting curiosities and other tidbits of information related to blessings and their recitation.

BLESSINGS RECITED ONLY ONE TIME A YEAR

There are five blessings that are each recited only once each year. They are as follows:

Birkat Chametz (Searching for Leaven)

The search for leaven before the Festival of Passover begins on the evening of the fourteenth of *Nisan,* following an elaborate cleaning of the house in preparation for Passover. The search is performed symbolically by deliberately placing crumbs of bread in several parts of the house and then discovering and sweeping them into a wooden spoon which is wrapped in cloth and burning in the morning of Passover eve. The formal search for leaven begins with this blessing:

Baruch ata Adonai Elohaynu melech haolam asher kidshanu bemitzvotav vetzivanu al bi'ur chametz.

Praised are You, Lord our God, Ruler of the Universe who has made us holy by His commandments and commanded us concerning the burning of the leaven.

On Seeing Blossoms for the First Time in the Year

This blessing is recited when one sees trees blossoming for the first time in the year:

Baruch ata Adonai Elohaynu melech haolam shelo chisar b'olamo davar, u-vara vo briyot tovot v'ilanot tovim l'hanot behem b'nai adam.

Praised are You, Lord our God, Ruler of the Universe who has withheld nothing from His world and who has created beautiful creatures and beautiful trees for mortals to enjoy.

Blessing Over the *Yom Kippur* Candles

When the Day of Atonement is ushered in with the candle blessing, the following special blessing is recited:

Baruch ata Adonai Elohaynu melech haolam asher kidshanu bemitzvotav vetzivanu lehadlik ner shel Yom HaKippurim.

Praised are You, Lord our God, Ruler of the universe who has made us holy by His commandments and commanded us to light the candles of the Day of Atonement.

Afternoon *Tisha B'av Amidah* Blessing – *Nachem*

The fast day of Tisha B'Av (Ninth of Av) commemorates the destruction of the Jerusalem Temples. In the afternoon of the Ninth of Av a special blessing is added to the Amidah which is recited only one time a year. The blessing praises God for comforting Zion and rebuilding Jerusalem:

Comfort, Lord our God, the mourners of Zion and those who grieve for Jerusalem, the city which once was so desolate in mourning, like a woman bereft of her children. For Your people Israel, smitten by the sword, and for her children who gave their lives for her. Zion cries with bitter tears and Jerusalem voices her anguish: 'My heart, my heart goes out for the slain. My entire being mourns for the slain.' Have mercy, Lord our God, in Your great compassion for us and for Your city Jerusalem, rebuilt from destruction and restored from desolation... Praised are You, Lord, who comforts Zion and rebuilds Jerusalem.

Blessing After the *Barechu* in the *Shacharit* (Morning) *Yom Kippur* Service

This special blessing recited on the morning of the Day of Atonement expresses gratitude to God for opening His gates of mercy.

> Praised are You, Lord our God, Ruler of the Universe, who opens for us the gates of mercy and lightens the eyes of them that hope for your forgiveness, who forms light and creates darkness, who makes peace and creates all things.

BLESSING ON SEEING 600,000 OR MORE JEWS TOGETHER

Some rabbis suggest that this blessing be recited on the arrival of the Messianic Era, when the Jewish people will be gathered together. Others posit that God's greatness lies in God's ability to know each and every person within a seemingly faceless crowd.

> *Baruch ata Adonai Elohaynu melech haolam chacham harazim.*

> Praised are You, Lord our God, Ruler of the universe, Knower of secrets.

BLESSING ON SEEING A FRIEND AFTER A LAPSE OF 12 MONTHS OR MORE

Friendship was valued in Talmudic times, and friends saw each other with great frequency. If a friend had not seen a friend for a year, it was likely a sign that his friend had died. That was the origin of this blessing which appears in the Talmud.

> *Baruch Ata Adonai mechayei hamayteem.*

> Praised are You, God, who revives the dead (*Talmud Berachot 58b*).

BLESSING BEFORE RETIRING AT
NIGHT (BEDTIME *SHEMA*)

The Bedtime *Shema* asks for peace and protection before one goes to sleep.

> Praised are You, Lord, Sovereign of the Universe, who closes my eyes in sleep and my eyelids in slumber. May it be Your desire, God of my ancestors, to grant that I lie down in peace and that I rise up in peace. Let my thoughts not upset me, nor evil dreams. May my family be perfect in Your sight. Grant me light, lest I sleep the sleep of death. Blessed are You, God, whose majesty gives life to the entire world. Hear O Israel, the Lord is our God, the Lord is One.

TRAVELER'S PRAYER

The Traveler's Prayer petitions God for safety on the journey.

> May it be Your will, O God, and the God of our ancestors that You lead us toward peace, guide us toward peace, and make us reach our desired destination for life, gladness, and peace. May You rescue us from the hand of every enemy, ambush, bandits, and evil animals along the way, and from all manner of punishments that assemble to come to earth. May You send blessing in our every handiwork and grant us grace, kindness, and mercy in Your eyes and in the eyes of all who see us. May You hear the sound of our supplication because You are God who hears prayer and supplication. Praised are You, God, who hears prayer.

BLESSING ON BUILDING A PROTECTIVE
RAILING AROUND ONE'S ROOF

It was a biblical obligation to protect persons from falling off of one's roof by building a guard rail (parapet). Here is the traditional blessing for installing the parapet:

> *Baruch ata Adonai Elohaynu melech haolam asher kidshanu bemitzvotav vetzivanu la'asote ma'akeh.*

Praised are You, Lord our God, Ruler of the Universe, who has made us holy by His commandments and commanded us to construct a parapet.

BLESSING FOR SEPARATING *CHALLAH*

In biblical times the *kohen* received a share of the *challah*, as an offering (*Numbers 15:18–21*). Since *challah* can no longer be observed as a priestly offering because of the destruction of the Jerusalem Temple, when baking bread, Jewish housewives are instructed to throw a small portion of the dough (the size of an olive) into the oven, and to say the following blessing:

> *Baruch Ata Adonai Elohaynu melech haolam asher kidshanu bemitzvotav vetzivanu lehafreesh challah meen ha'eesa.*

> Praised are You, Lord our God, Ruler of the Universe who has made us holy by His commandments and commanded us to separate challah from the dough.

BLESSING ON SEEING A DESTROYED SYNAGOGUE

This blessing acknowledges trust in God's judgement, even in time of loss.

> *Baruch Ata Adonai Elohaynu melech haolam dayan ha'emet.*

> Praised are You, Lord our God, Ruler of the universe, You are the True Judge.

BLESSING ON HEARING GOOD NEWS

This blessing attributes good fortune to God's goodness. One of God's names is *HaTov* (The Good One).

> *Baruch Ata Adonai Elohaynu melech haolam hatov ve'hamayteev.*

> Praised are You, Lord our God, Ruler of the Universe, who is good and does good.

BLESSING ON DONNING A NEW GARMENT OF SIGNIFICANT VALUE TO THE WEARER

This blessing encourages mindfulness of what we have and a reminder to clothe the naked.

> *Baruch Ata Adonai Elohaynu melech haolam malbeesh arumeem.*

> Praised are You, Lord our God, Ruler of the universe who clothes the naked.

BLESSING ON WEARING A *TALLIT*

The *tallit* (prayer shawl), worn during morning prayers, has specially knotted fringes that serve as reminders of God's *mitzvot* (commandments). Wearing the *tallit* symbolizes accepting responsibility for fulfilling the commandments.

> *Baruch Ata Adonai Elohaynu melech haolam asher kidshanu bemitzvotav vetzivanu le'heetatef batzitzit.*

> Praised are You, Lord our God, Ruler of the Universe who has made us holy by His commandments and commanded us to envelop ourselves with fringes.

BLESSINGS FOR BINDING *TEFILLIN*

Tefillin (sometimes called phylacteries) are cubic black leather boxes with leather straps. The boxes contain Hebrew parchment with the words of the *Shema*. They are worn on one's head and arm during weekday morning services, and symbolize binding oneself to God.

BLESSING FOR BINDING *TEFILLIN* ON ONE'S ARM

> *Baruch Ata Adonai Elohaynu melech haolam asher kidshanu bemitzvotav vetzivanu lehaniach tefillin.*

> Praised are You, Lord our God, Ruler of the Universe who has made us holy by His commandments and commanded us to put on tefillin.

BLESSING FOR DONNING *TEFILLIN* ON ONE'S HEAD

Baruch Ata Adonai Elohaynu melech haolam asher kidshanu bemitz-votav vetzivanu al mitzvat tefillin.

Praised are You, Lord our God, Ruler of the universe who has made us holy by His commandments and commanded us regarding the commandment of *tefillin*.

BLESSING AT THE CEMETERY

Those who have not visited a cemetery for thirty days recite this blessing upon arrival:

Praised are You, Lord our God, Ruler of the Universe who fash-ioned you with justice, nourished and sustained you with justice, took your lives with justice, knows the sum total of you all with justice, and will restore and resuscitate you with judgment. Praised are You, God, who revives the dead.

BLESSING FOR AFFIXING A *MEZUZAH*

A *mezuzah* is a receptacle that is affixed to the doorpost contain-ing parchment with the words of the *Shema*. It fulfills the Biblical command to 'write the words on the doorposts of your house. (*Deuteronomy 6:9*).

Baruch Ata Adonai Elohaynu melech haolam asher kidshanu bemitz-votav vetzivanu leekboah mezuzah.

Praised are You, Lord our God, Ruler of the Universe who has made us holy by His commandments and commanded us to affix a *mezuzah*.

AMEN

According to Jewish law, anyone who hears another person recite a blessing is required to respond *Amen* (so be it) upon its conclusion

(*Orach Chayim* 215:2). *Amen* is a fulfillment of the verse: 'When I proclaim the name of God, give glory to God' (*Deuteronomy* 32:3). Moses said to the Israelites, 'When I bless the name of God, you declare God's greatness by answering Amen.'

Kein Yehi Ratzon (May it Be God's Will)

When the Prayer Leader says the three sentences of the Priestly Blessing during the repetition of the *Amidah*, the congregational response is *kein yehi ratzon* rather than *Amen* because the Prayer Leader is not actually blessing the people.

When Not to Respond *Amen*

One does not respond *Amen* to a blessing that one recites oneself. The only exception to this rule is the third blessing in the Grace After Meals, when *Amen* is said to mark the end of the original Grace and thus becomes an integral part of the blessing's conclusion. It is also forbidden to respond amen to a blessing that is said needlessly and thereby takes the name of God in vain.

Premature *Amen*

Amen is said only after the blessing is entirely completed. The last syllables of the blessing must not be cut off by the response (*Orach Chayim* 124:8).

Orphaned *Amen*

One should not say *Amen* for a blessing that one does not actually hear and has no idea to what blessing they are responding. Such a response is called an 'orphaned *amen*' because it has no parent (*Orach Chayim* 124:8).

BLESSINGS ON TELEVISION AND RADIO

Some authorities have ruled that *Amen* is not said when a blessing is heard over radio or television. In light of the pandemic of 2020, other authorities have ruled that *Amen* should be said.

BLESSING BY A NON-JEW

A Jew who hears a blessing that is recited by a non-Jew may respond *Amen* (*Orach Chayim 215:2, Rema*).

BLESSING OVER FORBIDDEN FOOD

Maimonides ruled that one should not recite a blessing before or after eating forbidden food. However, his critic, the French Talmudist Abraham ben David disagreed, saying that a blessing should be recited before eating all food, kosher or unkosher.

GOD BLESS YOU

In early times Jews as well as other peoples believed that sneezing was the work of evil spirits determined to take a person's life. Jews have been known to respond to a sneeze with the verse that Jacob recited on his deathbed, 'For Your salvation have I hoped, O God' (*Genesis 49:18*) or by exclamations such as 'God bless you.'

Notable Blessing Quotations

Following are quotations about blessings culled from a variety of rabbinic sources.

- Rav Hamnuna Saba's blessing ran thus: May God keep His eye on you (*Zohar iv, 147b*).
- Thus shall you bless in the Holy tongue, in the fear of heaven and in humility (*Zohar iv, 145b*).
- There are treasures of life, of peace and of blessing (*Talmud Chagiga 12*).
- Israel enjoys blessings in this world because of the blessings of Balaam, but the blessings wherewith the Patriarchs have blessed them are preserved for the World-to-Come (*Midrash Deuteronomy Rabbah 3,4*)
- He who utters blessings is blessed; he who utters curses is cursed (*Ruth Rabbah 1,3*).
- The unrighteousness bring down curses upon the world, but the righteous bring blessings (*Zohar i, 87b*)
- With money earned across the sea, a man will never behold an omen of blessing (*Talmud Pesachim 3*).
- He who does not permit a scholar to share in the enjoyment of his property will have no blessing from it (*Talmud Sanhedrin 92*).
- Why was death the consequence of the census of Israel in the time of David? Because blessing does not attend a thing which is counted and numbered. And where there is no blessing, curses enter in (*Zohar ii, 187b*).

- The Rabbis asked: 'What is meant by the phrase "May the Lord bless you and watch over thee"?'
  - A Rabbi translated these words: 'May God bless you with sons and may God watch over your daughters' (*Midrash Numbers Rabbah 11,13*).
  - Another Rabbi translated these words: 'God will bless you with wealth and He will watch over you that with that wealth you shall perform *mitzvot*, good and beautiful deeds that shall redound to the glory of our God, to the honor and blessedness of our people' (*Midrash, Deuteronomy Rabbah 11,13*).
- Let not the blessing of a layman be light in your eyes (*Talmud Berachot 7*).
- From a man's blessings one may know if he be a scholar or not (*Talmud Berachot 50*).
- Just as one has to bless God for the good, one has to bless God for the bad (*Talmud Berachot 48*).
- There is no blessing save in what the eye sees not, or in what it masters not (*Talmud Taanit 8*).
- There is no blessing save if one stays in one place (*Talmud Taanit 8*).
- There is no vessel which holds blessedness more securely than peace (*Jerusalem Talmud Berachot 2,4*).
- When the Rabbis took their departure from the School of Rabbi Hanina, they said to him: 'May you see your world in this life; may your future be in the World to Come; may your name be remembered for many generations. May your heart perceive with understanding, may your mouth speak wisely, your tongue murmur melodiously, your eyebrows look straightforwardly, your eyes be kindled by the light of the Torah (*Talmud Berachot 17*).

Blessing Glossary

Anshay Knesset Hagedolah: Men of the Great Assembly who lived about 500–300 BCE (Before the Common Era). It is asserted that they helped to formulate many of the blessings known today.

Beracha Acharona: A condensed version of the Grace After Meals, recited whenever a person eats a minimum of one ounce by volume or drinks a minimum of three fluid ounces of any of the foods mentioned in the *Torah* as indigenous to the Land of Israel (*i.e.,* wine, grapes, figs, pomegranates, olives, dates. Also wheat, barley spelt, rye and oats whenever these grains are not in the form of bread).

Beracha ha-semucha le-chaverta: Contiguous blessing, where only the conclusion is phrased in the blessing style.

Beracha levatalah: Blessing recited in vain.

Birchot Hashachar: Blessings of the morning.

Birchot Hatorah: Blessings recited when one is honored with an *Aliyah* (being called up to the Torah.

Birkat Chametz: Blessing recited before searching for the leaven on the eve of Passover.

Birkat HaChodesh: Blessing of the new month, recited after the *Torah* reading on the Sabbath preceding the new month.

Birkat David: The fifteenth blessing of the daily *Amidah*, praising God for the coming of the Messiah.

Birkat HaGomel: Blessing offering to say thanks after recovering from a serious illness or returning from a voyage.

Birkat Halevana: New moon blessing, recited in the open air when the moon is visible between the fourth and the sixteenth of each month.

Birkat Hamazon: Grace After Meals.

Birkat Haminim: Twelfth blessing of the *Amidah*, praising God for breaking the power of His enemies.

Birkat Hamishpat: Eleventh blessing of the *Amidah*, petitioning God for the restoration of justice.

Birkat Hamotzi: Blessing over the bread.

Birkat Hashanim: The ninth blessing of the *Amidah*, petitioning God for economic prosperity.

Birkat Hatzadikkim: Blessing for the righteous, the thirteenth of the daily *Amidah*.

Birkat Hoda'ah: Blessing of thanksgiving.

Birkat Horim: Parental blessing by which some Jewish parents bless their children, notably on the eves of Sabbaths and Festivals.

Birkat Kohanim: Priestly blessing, expressed in three biblical verses from *Numbers 6:24–26* and chanted at the end of every *Amidah* prayer.

Birkat Nehenin: Blessings that encourage people to be mindful and to take nothing for granted. They encourage people to acknowledge the beauty of the world and all that sustains people, such as food and wonders of nature.

Birkat Sheva: The Sabbath *Amidah* is often called *birkat sheva* because it contains seven blessings.

Birkat Shalom: The nineteenth blessing of the daily *Amidah*, that expressed gratitude to God for blessing His people Israel with peace.

Birkat Yerushalayim: Blessing for the restoration of Jerusalem, the fourteenth blessing of the daily *Amidah*.

Matbe'ah Aroch: Longer formula of a blessing, in which the opening formula is followed by a more elaborate text.

Matbe'ah Katzar: Short formula of a blessing, which after its opening words of *Baruch Ata Adonai* is followed by a few words of praise specific to the occasion.

Sheva Berachot: Seven wedding blessings.

For Further Reading

Arian, Philip and Azriel Eisenberg. *The Story of the Prayerbook*. Hartford: Prayerbook Press, 1968.

Brown, Steven M. *Higher and Higher: Making Jewish Prayer a Part of Us*. New York: United Synagogue Department of Youth, 1979.

Donin, Hayim Halevy: *To Pray as a Jew*. New York: Basic Books, 1980.

Ganzfried, Hyman. *Code of Jewish Law*. (translated. by Hyman Goldin). New York: Hebrew Publishing Company, 1961.

Garfiel, Evelyn. *Service of the Heart. A Guide to the Jewish Prayerbook*. Northvale, New Jersey: Jason Aronson, 1989.

Grishaver, Joel. *And You Shall Be a Blessing:An Unfolding of the Six Words that Begin Every Brakhah.* Northvale, New Jersey: Jason Aronson, 1992.

Isaacs, Ron. *Count Your Blessings: One Hundred Prayers for a Day.* Jersey City: Ktav Publishing, 2004.

Millgram, Abraham. *Jewish Worship*. Philadelphia: Jewish Publication Society, 1971.